CHALLENGE
OF THE
TROUT

CHALLENGE OF THE TROUT

Gary LaFontaine

Illustrations by
Bill Elliott and Jeff Johnson

MOUNTAIN PRESS PUBLISHING CO.
Missoula, Montana 59801

Sections of this book have previously
appeared in the following magazines:
Angler Magazine,
Fly Fisherman Magazine,
The Flyfisher,
Roundtable.

Library of Congress Cataloging in Publication Data

LaFontaine, Gary J.
  Challenge of the trout.

  Bibliography: p.
    1. Trout fishing. I. Title.
SH687.L32   799.1'7'55   76-8608
ISBN 0-87842-058-4

TO DICK FRYHOVER...

...understanding friend and skilled fisherman, whose magic rod has often lured from subtle and obscure holding water the big browns and rainbows that other anglers miss.

Acknowledgments

In the preparation of this book, many people close to the author have offered invaluable knowledge and skill not only to the realm of trout fishing, but also in preparing the script for publication. The writer's deep appreciation and thanks go especially to the following:

To Stan Bradshaw, who shared an apprenticeship in the fundamentals of fly fishing.

To Ardyce LaFontaine, who helped edit the text with tact and insight.

To Bill Seeples, who patiently taught the author the value of underwater observation.

To the membership of the Connecticut Fly Fishermen's Association, whose fanatic love of trout fishing proved contagious.

To Browning, Cortland, Skyline, and Pflueger, who provided fine equipment for testing.

Foreword

I was jealous of Gary LaFontaine from the first day he came into our offices at Fly Fisherman Magazine — literally over the transom and unannounced — some six years ago. In his mid-twenties then, with a lovely wife and baby in tow, he had already made the transition from the home waters of his Connecticut youth to the heavier flows and wilder rewards of western Montana.

"Too much too soon," I kept muttering as he unfolded his private world of angling in that land to the west which boasts of fish to match its sky. A piscatorial late-bloomer myself, I had always felt that anyone under thirty should be kept off the better trout streams — and that, in the case of Montana waters, the age limit should be extended to the mid-forty age bracket.

But then, as communiques, calls, and articles began flowing in to us from Deer Lodge, Montana, a gradual metamorphosis began to occur, and I started to shed my nymphal shuck of prejudice. Jealousy turned to admiration, and Gary LaFontaine suddenly became a symbol to me of a new generation of anglers, young but distressingly mature in years astream, technically proficient, wildly curious, avid in their search for perfection, and a generation perfectly at one with that natural world to which the gentle art of the fly fisher is among the most ecologically acceptable keys of entry.

This crowd LaFontaine runs with, these Dharma bums of anglingdom, have frequently slipped slight-shod over the presentations of past masters selecting or rejecting offerings from fishing lore and literature with the same keen insights with which they search for trout. But they are not floating islands on the edge of the mainstream — they fish the subtle mini-currents and eddies within the same waters which have flowed past centuries of anglers. Although they have not found it necessary to stand on the shoulders of giants of the past (who loom less large to this new breed), they are not above peeking over giant shoulders occasionally. They know where to find something of value among the flotsam and jetsam.

For example, Gary gets right down to business in his discourse on meeting "the challenge of the trout." No fussing with fixtures. He moves directly on page 1 to that environment which controls the life of any angler, the water itself. It sometimes amazes me just how long it takes some angling writers to get there — and how others, after they finally make it down to the bank, seem to look upon the expanse before them as a great and sterile bathtub, apparently a medium primarily designed to support their flies. Poetically, yet with pinpoint accuracy, LaFontaine takes on his various waters one at a time, each with its inherent trickery — "The Mix of the River," "The Quiet of the Stream," "The Puzzle of a Spring-Creek,"and "The Lure of a Mountain Lake." How clearly each companion-word conjures the proper image — the many-faceted flows of a large river; the surprising complex of a stream's mini-currents; the inscrutable nature of cold- and clear-flowing spring waters; and the mystical draw of living, breathing high-mountain lakes.

There is something of the roué, usually more temperately directed than in reality, in any fly fisher, and family-man LaFontaine has managed to juggle a continuing love affairs with two mistresses, both waters and words. He treats them well and naturally, both as the living, flowing delights they are, and makes it easy for the reader to move from a stream or lake to the hard facts of our angling life — that fish do not make a habit of leaping into our arms, nets or canoes. We must defraud, of course, and in his section on the techniques of this at-once low and high pursuit, Gary makes is sound almost honest — even to the gay deceivers he finally commends to us after his closing section on the natural feeds of trout. We were pleased to see separate chapters on the natural caddis, the salmon fly, the grasshopper and the sculpin, as well as the traditional mayfly, for these have become more and more important to anglers during recent years.

There is a concern that the casual reader of this book's dust jacket might assume that this LaFontaine is just another "big fish-sky-water" angler (bless all the lucky dogs!) writing his memoirs, but that is further from the truth than even a fisherman might wander. Gary spent his fishing apprenticeship on the waters of Connecticut and the more intimate waters of the East, at least as many years of his angling life as he has enjoyed among the blue-ribbon streams of Montana and the Rockies. Anecdotal recounts of earlier times on Massachusett's Sudbury River intermingle comfortably with later tales of the Yellowstone.

Nor is what follows here scripture — truthfully, it is more the critical reminiscence and slightly premature confession of a still-growing angler, who has more to say than he could possibly contain without severe internal injury to himself. *Challenge of the Trout* is a book that had to be written.

If you're an Old Crud like me, read it in shame — and in a hurry. If you're one of those Young Turks, you'll read it no matter what I say.

But remember — within a few months of publication Gary LaFontaine will be over the hill. If you don't trust anyone over thirty, you can find some solace in the fact that the book was written in the author's twenty-ninth year.

Happy dotage, Gary! And thanks for making me feel young again for a few pages.

Don Zahner
Editor and Publisher
Fly Fisherman Magazine
Dorset, Vermont
August, 1976

Contents

Jeff Johnson

I
THE WATER

Chapter I

The Mix of the River

THE RIVER BROKE from a meandering course to enter a stretch of alternating rapids. The water rollicked among obstructing rocks, its fury discharging into deep pools suspended like steps of quiet in the flow. The current regathered at lips of the intermittent holes to rush in renewed haste down the slides of white water.

We had abandoned the unproductive flats during the morning and instead threaded a path deep to the boil-heads of the Deschutes River. We plucked reluctant trout by hitting still patches in the churning tumble, but we quit the area before noon because of the exhaustion of standing in the rips.

Brian Winship huffed as we crossed, "Is the river mean enough for you?"

The shove of current pressured my return steps into a half-hour of teetering ballet. "We'll come back."

"Why not?" he laughed. "We're fools enough."

Brian probed with a wading staff, pushing into the flow and struggling among an array of boulders. He dapped with his long nine-foot rod, skittering a dry Hornberg in the prime lanes behind each rock. With diligent coverage of the foam, he pulled a fussing 20-inch brown to the hop of the fly.

The triumph was fair testament to the efficacy of fishing a suitable stretch of rapid water; in the doldrums of mid-day heat, the wide and slick flats shimmered lifeless, yielding nothing to the efforts of uncompromising fly casters flailing the quieter water of each pool.

The dry fly method was a rigidly codified art on the chalk streams of England. On those historic waters prolific emergences of *Ephemeroptera* challenged the angler to cast to rising trout; and by set rules of propriety, the fly was cast only to visibly feeding fish.

The transplant of the dry fly to this country fostered a different brand of purism. On the freestone rivers of the charmed circle of the Catskills — Willowemoc, Beaverkill, Rondout, Esopus, Neversink — fly fishermen adapted theories to particular necessities of the water. No longer were casts proffered only to the rise; it was too possible to view the tumble of mountain water all day without marking an active fish. The restrictions of English practice were replaced by the speculative angling of a prospecting fly.

The Dry Fly & Fast Water, by George M. LaBranche, explained to an angling public the technique of "fishing the water":

> This [the white water] is the difficult water to fish with the dry fly, and many anglers believe it to be quite impossible. If the dry fly...is placed properly and with due calculation, it is as easily kept dry and floating as upon any other part of the stream. The explanation lies in the fact that the fly is not placed directly upon the white water at all, if it be properly placed, but is cast to either side of the swift water, always on the side nearest the angler first, who should pick out the smooth looking spots upon which to place the fly. The fish...are taken on the dry fly by being

4

induced to move out of their position. A very short line is used, and the fly is floated but a foot or two, being dropped lightly again and again.

The water demands this "pick-pocket" approach when the stream surface presents a blank sheet. With no indication of rising or nymphing trout, the fisherman covers the flow in search of action. The fly is proffered to points suspected of holding fish, the drift playing to the spot as if each cast were performing to an assured audience; and it is most difficult for the beginning fly caster to feel the confidence that insures concentration.

On blank water there is a noticeable difference in the approach of the expert fly fisherman, who is consistently successful, and the unskilled fly fisherman, who is typically frustrated: the successful angler casts the fly to somewhere, and the unskilled angler casts the fly to anywhere.

On the riffles, presentation to precise holding spots becomes more important than an imitative fly, and thus a pattern that matches a prevalent insect is not necessarily the most successful. Visibility of the artificial to both trout ahd angler stands as a simple judgment for usage.

From the view of fish, choppy water acts like a fragmented mirror as it distorts light penetration. Air bubbles further create an effect that diminishes the upward cone-vision of trout into a flourescent haze. Portions of a floating object projecting above the skin of surface film are not readily visible from below, and primary recognition is provided by the body bulk pressed down through the meniscus.

An underwater contrast-photograph of two dry flies easily illustrates the point: a fly drifting flush is clearly defined through the surface confusion, but an alternate pattern riding high on sparse hackle points is lost in glare.

Many bulky patterns are designed for fast water as attractor creations, but actually in the fractured chop of a riffle, these flies appear neither gaudy nor over-sized. In turbulence, the patterns

5

simulate vulnerable prey with a silhouette that excites a trout into a hurried curiosity attack.

Often it proves difficult to convince visiting anglers that these bulk patterns are serious tools on Western rivers, but these "atrocities" even fool trout on stretches of steep-gradient streams all over the country.

For the dry fly purist, this riffle-chugging grows to an art. It develops into a game, the pattern slipping over a specific patch of dark water, with the objective of repeating the exact drift enough times to draw fish from rest-holds to a position of feeding readiness.

"On a lazy day, I never fish anything except a dry fly," Perry Donovan said during an afternoon on the Bitterroot River, "and they're all lazy days."

I offered a deer-body pattern, "Try this."

"That's not a fly," he grinned; "that's a battleship."

He refused to believe the reliability of out-size patterns for this rough water, but he switched from general No. 12-14 flies after catching a passel of small trout from the current creases. When he finally cut back the leader tippet, he picked out the largest Rat-Faced McDougall in the box. He slapped the No. 4 deer-hair monstrosity on the water and watched it wobble for a moment before it vanished in an eruption of spray.

A trout churned towards the depth of the upstream pool, splashing in resplendent fury in the upper riffle. When it failed to reach cover, it bucked against the fast water and the rod. The beaten fish drifted back with the flow.

Perry primped the sodden McDougall pried from the maw of the 4-lb. rainbow. "A perfect match for a natural," he insisted puckishly.

"Maybe for a dead bird," I conceded.

It is during periods of bright sun, when light-sensitive trout

6

hide in the depths or in the shade, that tumbling currents continue to hold fish in shallows. Water action supplies the requisites of food, aeration, and cover, and in zones of quiet behind buffers, fish lie in easy comfort.*

The force of flow diminishes near the bottom of a stream and leaves ideal niches. Each jut from the bed acts as a deflector to split the current into varying ribbons of velocity, forming creases of relative calm between the lanes.

On Mill Brook a particular brute brown trout staked the area behind a mid-current boulder, chasing off the more common 7 to 11 inch intruders. During non-active moments the fish sank snug to the dead water directly at the rear of the stone, but to feed it dropped back four feet and sidled next to the main flow. It poked only a snout into the faster rips to nuzzle any drift-trapped specks of life.

I often perched on a high bank watching the first afternoon mayflies struggle to emerge. I noticed the trout begin to edge away from the stone only after 20 or 30 insects followed each other down the lane.

During summer many fly fishermen splashed up behind that feeding slot. Usually they scattered three or four random pecks in general eddies of the rock, missing the precise band of the active position and failing to repeat the number of full drifts required to lure the fish into the spot.

A river strange to a man is a flow of minor peculiarities. Twists and curls of the current that buffet a fly or hide a trout are unseen by a cursory glance. Even areas of fish-promise conceal a multitude of subtle truths.

The angler exploring the promise of a river studies the water: the water as hindrance to the fish, with the push and swirl of

---

*Riffles are the biologic larders of the trout stream, generating approximately 80% of the total invertebrate life. Browsers gather algae clinging to rocks or detrital litter, filter-feeders strain particles swimming in the drift, hunters seek insect prey hiding among crevices. Clinging, swimming, and crawling forms of life share the distinctive habitat of shallow gravel.

7

current restricting the trout's holding area; the water as a convenience to the fish, with the flow and eddy of current delivering the trout's natural food.

Within the environment of a stream, the activity of trout is ordered mostly by three determining influences, in effect a linked triangle:

- prevailing condition of the weather
- availability pattern of the natural feed
- flow characteristic of the water

No factor acts singly upon the fish, but at moments one of the determinants may serve as the primary control. The varying structure of these interdependent forces defines a trout's scope of feeding: where, when, what, how, and why.

Each variance of these natural phenomena affects the method and manner of the fly fisherman. The angler plies the river differently according to the conditions that prevail upon the fish, conditions that dictate the choice of fly presented in a certain manner to a selected spot.

The trout is a relatively simple creature reacting to stimuli in a basic pattern of response; thus the fascination of angling for the fly fisherman must lie in the infinite variables of environment that subtly shift the activity of the fish.

N. Tinbergen, Scientific American, December, 1952

The sex life of the three-spined stickleback (*Gasterosteus aculeatus*) is a complicated pattern, purely instinctive and automatic, which can be observed and manipulated almost at will.

In nature, sticklebacks mate in early spring in shallow fresh waters. The mating cycle follows an unvarying ritual, which can be seen equally well in the natural habitat or in tanks. First, each male leaves the school of fish and stakes out a territory for itself, from which it will drive any intruder, male or female. Then it builds a nest. It digs a shallow pit in the sand bottom, carrying the sand away mouthful by mouthful. When this depression is about two inches square, it piles in a heap of weeds, preferably thread algae, coats the material with a sticky substance from its kidneys and shapes the weedy mass into a mound with its snout. It then bores a tunnel in the mound by wriggling through it. The tunnel, slightly shorter than an adult fish, is the nest.

Having finished the nest, the male suddenly changes color. Its normally in-conspicuous gray coloring had begun to show faint pink blush on the chin and a greenish gloss on the back and in the eyes. Now the pink becomes a bright red and the back turns a bluish white.

In this colorful, conspicuous dress the male at once begins to court females. They, in the meantime, have also become ready to mate - their bodies have grown shiny and bulky with 50 to 100 large eggs. Whenever a female enters the male's territory, he swims toward her in a series of zigzags - first a sideways turn away from her, then a quick movement toward her. After each advance the male stops for an instant and then performs another zigzag. This dance continues until the female takes notice and swims toward the male in a curious head-up posture. He then turns and swims rapidly toward the nest, and she follows. At the nest, the male makes a series of rapid thrusts with his snout into the entrance. He turns on his side as he does so and raises his dorsal spines toward his mate. Thereupon, with a few strong tail beats, she enters the nest and rests there, her head sticking out from one end and her tail from the other. The male now prods her tail base with rhythmic thrusts, and this causes her to lay her eggs. The whole courtship and egg-laying ritual takes only about one minute. As soon as she has laid her eggs, the female slips out of the nest. The male then glides in quickly to fer-tilize the clutch. After that he chases the female away and goes looking for another partner.

One male may escort three, four or even five females through the nest, fer-tilizing each batch of eggs in turn. Then his mating impulse subsides, his color darkens and he grows increasingly hostile to females. Now he guards the nest from predators and "fans" water over the eggs with his breast fins to enrich their supply of oxygen and the fish spends more time ventilating them. The ventilating reaches a climax just before the eggs hatch. For a day or so after the young emerge, the father keeps the brood together, pur-suing each straggler and bringing it back in his mouth. Soon the young sticklebacks become independent and associate with the young of other broods.

Chapter 2

The Quiet of the Stream

THE OLD HIGHWAY passed through the hills in a twisting two-lane ribbon. A scattering of white shingle-board houses sat behind wide bumpy lawns of groomed dandelions. Rural post boxes perching next to intermittent driveways broke the landscape of trees and fields.

At the cement-bridge pool, a rise to the minutiae of midge flourished for brief intervals each evening. The drift of pupae roused trout to sip with fastidious choosiness in the muted light, and any approach required a studied delicacy as the flats of the river flowed in a spell of teasing dimples.

"Does anybody fish there?" the man on the lawn chair groused. "Sure...too many — always parking cars that squeeze out the road."

In the stream the flush of *Chironomidae* pupae strayed helpless with vagaries of the current, the profuse olive midges suspended from breathing gills anchored in the meniscus. By sheer number the tiny fare drew even wary trout nose-tight to the surface.

At the back-water of an oval pool, a particular trout sipped steadily, feeding with graceful efficiency in the shimmer and leaving a necklace of bubbles on the minor current of the Jeremy's River.

The solitary fish held in the difficult notch of an eddy, where a cast line flopped across opposing currents. Even with the snake-loops of a loose leader, slack paid out too quickly for any effective drift. The drag snatched the fly unnaturally to tip the fraud of imitation.

With grease covering the leader except for the final 18 inches of tippet, most of the connection floated; however, the untreated portion of nylon enabled the No. 22 Olive Midge Pupa to hang in the current just under the surface in simulation of a natural insect. A limp section of 7X monofilament enhanced the free movement of the sunken pattern.

After three evenings of failing to reach the trout, I finally solved the problem of drag by edging too far down the slope of the hole. As I crept deeper to overcome the boggling divisions of flow, I felt cold seepage over the top of my chest waders; I pushed closer, despite frigid trickles running inside the canvas, and dropped the fly beyond the compounding direction of the near current.

Two boys with bicycles stopped to peer over the bridge railing. "Mister, what're you doing?"

I shivered hard in the chill, standing in water above my armpits. "I'm going to catch this fish."

"You're getting wet," they taunted, and peddled away.

The sharp tatter of a woodpecker pocked along with a twilight chorus of crickets. Chub and small trout mustered in shallow flats of the pool to spatter the panning lip. Scurrying animals darted along the river banks during that beauty of dusk-gloom peculiar to an Eastern forest.

I stared at the point where the leader dropped into the water, the floating segment of nylon snaking in an opaque ribbon on the

10

drift. I glimpsed a slight downward-bending curl and set the hook.

The trout shook into the air with a frantic partial twist. In the restricted pool — the shallow riffles both above and below the area offered no haven of exit — the fish zipped with determined rushes against the tiny hook planted in the bone of his jaw.

I slogged with clumsy steps from the river, stooping with the trapped heft of the water. Slipping off the suspender straps, I leaned to empty my waders in a gush onto the gravel. I pulled the feet free to kick off the soggy boots.

The 17-inch brown trout followed the coax of the rod to swim near a sand bar, wallowing on one side as gills worked in futile haste to dispel exhaustion. It slid meekly onto the beach on the next pass.

I lifted the fish for the release; a splendid specimen for a stream as small as the Jeremy's River — the only trout over 13 inches I caught in Connecticut that summer.

In a simplified view of a freestone stream, the water is divided into riffle and pool. A riffle, or a rapids, is a movement of current agitated as it contacts the rock strata. A pool, or a flat, is a distribution of the flow-energy dissipated over an enlarged square/measure area. Each type serves a specific value to the trout capacity of a stream.

A pool is a settling basin. As the current spreads into the area, drift-fare held in suspension is deposited by the flow. At the drop-point, where insects of greater bulk filter from the current, the hold is a gathering place for trout which pick out the stranded nymphs; here fish often feed selectively on the prevalent species of nymph in the drift.

Trout abandon recesses of deep water when an emergence of aquatic insects or a fall of terrestrial insects stimulates the rise in a pool. Then feeding positions of the fish trace the channel of current through the basin.

The movement of water, splitting into bands of varying speed, serves as a conveyor to present the vulnerable insects. At the head

11

of the inflow, in the swirl of an eddy or at the lip of an outflow, the current gathers struggling fare on the surface or in the film.

Many fly fishermen approach pool water as if it were in the uniform slope of a bowl with a straight flow-through of current. Casts are merely impatient pecks at the edge or at the riffle-head, without any particular concentration of effort.

But a pool consists of varying bottom structure. Each obstruction and each depression provides the safety of cover for a trout. Exposed patches seldom hold prime fish during the bright part of the day, unless an emergence of insects moves the trout to forage in open water.

The knack of reading a pool requires an ability to correlate current with structure. Where the line of flow intercepts the deepest tangle, the best trout typically hold. If the pool offers several such areas, then the one with the heaviest over-drop of feed carries the bull fish of the water.

As a fisherman reads the bottom, he weighs the balancing triad of influences that determine fish activity, each of which moderates the value of the other:

- weather condition
- water type   - insect activity

The penetration angle and intensity of sunlight largely determine the potential of structure. A morning sun strikes the water opposite from the afternoon sun, casting shade in a different direction and shifting the cover zones of trout. An overcast day that diffuses the light or a windy day that chops the surface makes depth of cover less critical.

The prime feeding areas of a pool depend on insect activity. A mating fall of caddis flies spatters a flat panning of water with random drops, causing fish to cruise under the surface. An emergence migration of stone flies crawling along "clambering

12

paths" lines rocks of the edges to tempt trout to hunt over the shallows.

As a fly fisherman studies the intricacies of a river, the secrets of the insect cycle tattle on the trout. Natural accumulations of feed dictate concentrations of fish so that the angler anticipates shifts of activity to specific portions of a stream.

I pointed out a prime hold in a stretch of the upper Clark Fork to Don Traffley and Gary Buttle, "On a slow river like this, the browns stack at deep curves, not at the shelves of pools."

In wind that whipped over the stream, the casting of a beginner proved justifiably sloppy. "That's a bad spot," Don groaned as the Wooly Worm plopped in a few inches of water.

When he lifted the rod to start another cast, the shaft bent downwards. The glass bowed in an ever-increasing hoop until the heavy leader snapped, a large fish kicking free upstream.

"That bugger wasn't supposed to be there," I fussed.

We abandoned Don to his glory-hole, while we wandered to the big flats of the river. "I don't suppose," Gary smiled with puckish humor, "that I'm going to try these shallows."

"That one might have been a fluke."

"Think so?"

The rain fell in the driven spatter of a spring chill. A patch of clouds blanketed the sun, an aura of light spreading around the intervening cloud-mass; minor rainbows shimmered on the horizon. But in that fiery rosetta-pink of sky, the day still held a biting cold.

We kept warm by pursuing fish we plucked from the shallows. On the dark Wooly Worm we hauled brown trout in mad profusion, on any cast hooking an eager battler even before the fly settled to the bottom.

"I'm glad you decided it was all right to fish in close," Gary teased, "because I never do any good when I disagree with you."

When the mystery of the "near" trout proved too much to leave unanswered, I ruined a piece of good water by wading into the edge. I squatted next to the flow to peer at the litter of the bottom, stirring

13

the muck with a stick to scare any life-forms into a disclosing swim.

Along the sunken leaf piles of the shallows, nymphs of the green damselfly clung just under the surface, the insects edging onto the moist tops of weed bunkers. So many of the transforming adults rested at the rim of vegetation that the algal scum throbbed with the blend of the living mass.

Back at the original place, Don sat in dejected confusion, telling tales of smashed tippets and straightened hooks, "Aren't there any small fish here?"

The windy weather and abundant insect activity of that day had combined to alter the usual holding patterns of fish in the pools. Under the influence of two determining factors, the trout forsook the safety and convenience of trace-current lies.

Later, when the afternoon bloomed in spotty sunshine, these margins of the river stood devoid of bigger fish. Even though numerous damselfly nymphs continued to hatch, none of the 15 to 20 inch fish lingered to cruise the edges. Only fading light of dusk returned the shy brown trout to the shallows.

Although the differences appear obvious between flat water and rough water in the pool/riffle division of a freestone stream, a basic mistake in fly fishing is unthinking coverage of both habitats in an identical manner.

Slow currents require pattern-types with an imitative allure. Clearly visible in the flow, a wet fly needs responsiveness to the gentle force of the water. On the surface a dry fly demands realistic interpretation of insect light-pattern.

Even more important than fly choice is the time-efficiency of angling rhythm: too slow an approach to broken currents wastes time, and too hasty an approach to calm flows spooks fish — each separate stream feature dictates a change in casting pace.

On riffles the cycles of blind casting to productive spots proceeds efficiently with quick pops to the trout. "There are two places a fly can be," Dick Fryhover keeps repeating, "in the air or on

14

the water. And it'll never catch a fish in the air."

This dictum partially explains the mastery of an expert over a stream. No one covers a patch of water with less superfluous movement. With fluid casting, Fryhover virtually strips away every secret of holding potential — and with the fly probing the water as much as 15% to 25% longer than the pattern of a typical fly fisherman, there naturally exists greater opportunity for fooling trout.

But the approach rhythm alters in covering a pool. Here, a too enthusiastic flogging of the water proves harmful. Due to the spookiness of trout, the initial cast to each distinct piece of pool structure becomes the most important moment of presentation. A cautious stalk ensures the chances of a suitable fly.

On the Rapidan River of Virginia, the water tumbles in a procession of smooth pockets, the stream emptying from slate-rock gorges into pools of limpid clarity. Along the sides, a brushy clutter of hardwood forest crowds the shallows.

Nathan Dulice hosted an angling day on this favored river, the professor from the University even refusing to carry a fly rod himself. "At the end of summer," he explained, as we followed the path along the water, "these trout are so wary on this fish-for-fun stretch that only one man can work each spot."

With the skill of an accomplished sunk-pattern fly fisherman, he read the bottom of the stream as if no surface currents obscured his vision. He ignored all the distracting shadow and distortion of the water to notice only significant features of the rock jumble.

"Are you sure you won't fish?" I pressed.

"I'll be fishing every time you cast," he smiled.

"Who says this isn't a spectator sport?"

I ruined the first few pools through undue haste, in my boldness sending trout scurrying for deeper cover even before the faint splash of line; but with a renewed vow of stealth, I studied the next upstream patch of holding area before barging into the angling act.

Nat watched the bungling with a generous silence. "Very low

15

water this year," he finally added.

In those hummock mountains of the Allegheny range, the land attains a wild aspect in isolated niches away from the road. As the lush blooms of flowering bushes pass, the vegetation packs densely into a camouflage assembly of varying shades of green.

I paused purposely, while stalking the water, to listen to the call of a bird and gaze at the scamper of a squirrel. I adopted deliberate movements against the drab background of foliage; clad in matching green vest and dark clothing, I masked any betraying motion.

Nat aided as an experienced spotter. "You're in a beautiful position for a cast to that long depression near the head."

I tossed a tiny caddis pupa pattern far enough above the slot of stones for a leisurely sink to the level of the trout. After mending with minor corrections to let the fly dance unhindered down within the fish-hold, I raised my arms overhead in the slow draw of the "Leisenring" lift.

One of the grey forms of the bottom broke free to trail the pupal pattern to the surface, finally busting the artificial with a swirl that tore the placid water. In a dive back to the depression, the frenzied fighter scattered an entire pod of lunker rainbows.

Nat slipped the hook from the mouth of the spent fish. "I'm afraid he spoiled this water for a while."

We proceeded to further stretches, where the soft breath of animation with a pattern — a ploy named for the late James Leisenring — plucked both rainbow and brook trout. We planned the specific moment of the fly-rise, kicking the fly into life at prime spots.

In the evening we laughed about the botched water at the start of the day. "I always do the same thing at the beginning," Nat mused, "so I fish at first in poor potholes — nothing over 10 inches there — until I settle down to the quietness all over again."

The angling proved very much in touch with the underwater world in this open environment. With the long vision of deep-lying

16

trout, every nuance for deception needed reasoned attention, such as positioning a blinding sun at the back of the angler. These natural factors of concealment redeemed the careful fly fisherman.

In a consideration of stream habitat, a realistic angling approach narrows to an either/or selection — a choice of casting the water of preference or casting the pattern-type of preference; in either case the fly fisherman benefits from the dual character of a freestone river.

A purist determined to ply a dry pattern with success divides his attention between pool and riffle. During moments of rise, the flat water offers a fair challenge for an imitative technique. For dead periods of blank surface, chop water presents an opportunity for the searching method.

But the angler concentrating solely on the fussy pools of a stream fits the manner of approach to the necessities of the situation. The dry fly proves valuable only when fish hold in a position near enough to the surface to notice the pattern. When trout retreat deep into a pool, the sunken fly provides the means for a favorable effort.

These flat-water portions require knowledge of a river's rhythm. Without a sense of timing to place the fly fisherman at the prime spot at the right moment, flurries of activity often pass in unobserved brevity. Trout in pools respond to each minor shift of environmental influences too rapidly for random experimentation.

Chapter 3

The Puzzle of a Spring Creek

VAN McGINNIS peered at the silk mix of currents, "What's a dub like me doing here?"

"A day on a spring-creek is like a baptism," Fred Rapp clucked. "In spite of the tears, it does wonders for the soul."

At the rim of a bunker of weeds, a trout sipped an insect from the flow. The visible fish hung suspended above a bed of *Elodea* as it nosed the surface in gentle rhythmical feeding that pushed out rise-forms of concentric half-circles in no more than wrinkles.

"Anyway," I offered, "this water makes us all look like beginners."

Van approached slowly to a kneeling position, but as he false-cast, passes of line hovered over the rise spot and spooked the fish. "Too tough for me."

Fred consoled his pupil, "No. Just hold the line in close, but then shoot only the last cast to reach. That first real cast is the most important."

"Go ahead."

Fred edged towards a rising trout, a squat angler waddling in the epitome of stealth, and plopped a No. 16 Beetle precisely in the lane of drift. He whooped as the fish accepted the fly. "Nothing but luck," he protested too modestly.

A web of shade criss-crossed the stream with lengths of many-limbed trees. Rose bushes and weeping willows crowded water-side puffs of cress. In the overgrown meadow, the flowage meandered within a crimped channel of only 25 feet.

Enough fish rose to keep the group flush in opportunities, but after we separated to explore portions of the stream, the once-successful Beetle pattern failed. The fly passed untouched even when we felt certain no unnatural drag marred a float.

We commiserated as we passed, "These fish are busy on a no-calorie diet."

I snipped off each pattern in the process of refining the end tackle towards a more realistic match of the minutiae of the drift, the skimmings of ants and leaf-hoppers, in an inevitable abandonment of more comfortable tippets and hook sizes.

With a No. 22 Jassid on a 7X leader-point, I cast an upstream loop to a feeder sipping snug against the grass. I barely reacted in time as the fly vanished without a discernable rise, but the tiny hook bit firmly into the upper jaw of a trout as I lifted the rod tip.

Midget patterns never reduced angling to an easy affair; but if the approach and cast were perfect, the fish at least accepted the fly. With the Jassid we landed two more brown trout and ticked the flesh without penetration on many risers.

Fred resolutely cast the No. 16 Beetle; amazingly for an angler of his skill at presentation, he hooked not a single fish on the pattern. After he begrudgingly knotted on No. 20 and No. 22 flies, the trout acceded to the "wizard."

I returned to a pocket off a jutting clump of grass, replaying the drift of a diverging squibble of current with a slacker leader. I leaned forward to extend the float barely enough for a trout to suck down a No. 22 Cinnamon Ant.

The fish bore upstream between trailings of weed. It dallied only a moment in the channel before indulging in messy scrounging amidst the vegetation, dragging ribbons of scum on the leader knots and once burying in a pile of drifted cress.

At an opportune moment, I forced the tiring fish down to the sweep of the bend and lifted the rod to reel the feebly slapping trout over the weedy edge. I reached down the leader to snap the fly off rather than fuss with digging a buried hook from the mouth of the fish.

As a culmination to a "rookie" day on this stream, the husky brown trout of 18 inches taken on a midge pattern stood more highly prized than larger fish on other waters. "That'll make him a bit tougher next time."

"There aren't many dumb ones as it is," Fred grumbled.

Slight wonder that the days on the Letort Spring Run became as much a pilgrimage as a fishing expedition. Romantic expectation had hallowed the water, and we approached with a committed reverence — gypsy anglers imbued with an accumulation of legend.

It is easy to envy local anglers who study the vagaries of the Letort Spring Run; if the sly trout are not then any less mysterious, they are at least part of a familiar mystery on this most difficult of schools for a fly fisherman.

On limestone jewels of the Cumberland Valley, the techniques and the fly patterns of history were shunted aside in frustration because they did not produce with the holdover trout. These spring-run waters were the inspiration for the studies of an iconoclastic breed of angling geniuses.*

It was *A Modern Dry Fly Code,* by Vincent Marinaro, that detailed the experiments leading to new concepts of artificial pat-

———

*This was the notable group described in the writings of Carles Fox and Vincent Marinaro.

21

terns, flies representing types of insects seldom deemed important: the abundant terrestrials. These theories of imitation, so alien to past fly fishing practice, set the *Code* alone as the most innovative work in American angling literature, a book of importance beyond the confines of the limited geographical area of the Pennsylvania limestone shield and indispensable for approaching trout of any spring-water habitat.

The indentation of land-insects differs on the water from the dainty ride of a mayfly dun. The hackle of a conventional dry fly only distorts the desired silhouette and light pattern, so in radical departure from accepted fly dressing theory, Marinaro eliminated the hackle support. With flush patterns, he attained the opacity of a solid body-form drifting in the manner of a natural insect mired in the meniscus.

With the Jassid imitation of the minute leaf-hopper *(Cicadellidae)*, it was not necessary to represent the bulk of the insect. The nail of jungle cock feather flat over the trimmed bed of hackle fibers provided a suitable illusion of body-depth.

Before the development of effective terrestrial patterns, moments of the dry fly were limited to the abundance of early mayfly hatches. By midsummer the water was abandoned to uncatchable sipping risers. A core of ardent devotees remained to decipher the flaunt of feeding trout, until a solution to the terrestrial mystery extended angling days to the end of the legal season.

I served an apprenticeship on the spring creeks of Montana, using a copy of the *Code* to puzzle late-season problems common to these pastoral habitats, pondering emergences of miniature mayflies and falls of ubiquitous terrestrials that rigidly pattern the feeding response of trout in these alkaline streams.

With fare so rich in the sub-surface environment, trout of the spring-waters seldom rose in random fashion. Deep in weed beds, the fish nosed for abundant olive scuds and sow-bugs. At the edges of the channels, they picked off swimming mayfly nymphs and free-crawling caddis larvae.

Possibly the autocratic dictum of Frederick Halford for the chalk-streams of England was justifiable: "Fish the dry fly" — for truly it was easy to assume that these ideal flows had been created precisely for the pleasure of the dry fly angler.

And yet for a group of anxious fly fishermen on Benhardt Creek who wished to accomplish more than an idle span on the bank, there was nothing to do but to imitate the prevalent underwater life. The delicately cast nymph pattern promised the sole opportunity to break riseless moments.

Ron George carefully honed the hook point of a No. 18 Trueblood Otter Nymph, accepting the choice of the fly along with the offered services of a ghillie. "We'll use nymphs if we 'must," he acceded.

"We don't fish blind," I assured this closet purist. "Let's look for trout."

"And then what?"

We paced along the bank, carefully studying the windings of the channel. "Do you see those shadows at the curve of the weed bed?"

"I see two of them."

"Pitch the fly about three feet above the top one."

After soaking the pattern in spittle, he cast the nymph to sink perfectly in front of the lead fish. Noticing the turn of the trout to suck in the fly, he jerked the barb to a solid bite and deftly pressured the scrapper away from the pressing snags.

For Ron, this stalking of visible fish — Frank Sawyer method — proved a diverting occupation during the afternoon; but for the other clients, the game developed into a frustration of unseen quarry and unseen strikes.

Melinda George waved a fly rod with the refined smoothness of a training school graduate. After a 3-day course on a pond, she gracefully executed the casting stroke, but the application of class-learning to trout fishing remained a jumble of uncorrelated information.

The cool breeze of evening carried an initial fall of flying ants to the water. "Now, Melinda," I boasted, relishing the promise of easier dry fly action, "you're going to catch a fish."

The water gathered such a speckle of the minute ants that it flowed with an apparent layer of cinnamon dust. Hidden trout materialized to spatter the surface with rises. With rain-drop intensity, gentle rings crowded each flat sheet of the stream.

Norton Meagher clinched on a No. 10 Grey Wulff. He glanced towards me, "No use trying to match the natural when there are so many on the water. I'll show them something different" — a theory that works on rare occasions on freestone streams.

I picked out the rhythm of a fish working the swirl-edge of an eddy. Within the timing of 10-second feeding intervals, I touched the No. 22 Cinnamon Ant on the drift. Twice I lifted falsely as the fish plucked the surface within hair-breadths of the fly. Then the trout nabbed the artificial from among the glut of naturals. After a premature leap, it circled slowly with the current of the backwater. "Hey, Norton."

"Did you get a fish on that little bit of a fly?"

The trout bolted down the channel, arching in jumping-jack flops on the hurdling run, slamming into a bunker of shallow weeds where it buried in immobilized tail-wagging. After I booted it free, the fish splashed to exhaustion in the open water.

Melinda arrived with a net for the 4-pound brown. "I came back because I need another fly," she explained. "I just lost a fish about twice that big."

I answered, stifling any skepticism, "Really?"

"Right down there near that log."

Norton still randomly popped the garish Wulff pattern on the creases of the main flow. He slammed the fly on dissipating rings of rising fish. Although the trout never spooked, he abandoned each position in a flustered rush to more promising dimples.

"Did you try an ant?" I asked him.

24

"I couldn't even see one of those things on the water."

"Is that what you've been worried about?"

I snipped the Grey Wulff and replaced it with a fur-bodied Cinnamon Ant, which featured a white spike-wing in the center of a parachute hackle to enhance the visibility of the flush-drifting pattern without detracting from its quality.

"That stands right out," he agreed.

"Now just cast it by the end of that tree stump. Don't worry about any rises. Just keep the fly covering the same line of drift."

Repeatedly Norton floated the Ant past the jutting log. He bisected the sips of a solitary trout that worked with rapidly efficient surface tipping; with an accurate cast he linked the pass precisely with the expected rise.

Melinda and Ron ambled up. "Watch out," Ron grinned, "there's supposed to be a monster in that hole."

When it sucked the tiny hook, the trout swirled in a roll of golden flank, as a massive tail split the water, curling off diverging eddies; the fish casually peeled the leader through the snags.

Norton muttered repeatedly, "Goddamn."

"And you guys didn't believe me," Melinda chided.

Appearing grey in the cloud-cast light of evening, the face of the man sagged with drawn despondency, the sharp angles of his features fading to weakened softness. The wrinkles of his jowls lapped over the line of the jaw.

"Who would have thought a fish like that," Norton finally broke the silence during the walk to the truck, "would take such a tiny bit of fluff?"

We commiserated on the loss of the immense brown, "Ants do funny things to trout."

The break-off of the fish marked a fitting end to a day of fussy angling. With the accord of the group, we repaired to a bar in Bozeman to revive the spirits of a friend, and cheer even a brief hook-up of the resident bully brown.

The seep-lands of Montana are a paradise for the spring creek fancier. Alkaline flows are innumerable, issuing from rims of hill meadows to lace the valleys with trout-flush streams. A few of these creeks are famed for free-rising fish — Armstrong Spring or Nelson Spring — but there are less publicized springs in the state that are equally rich in trout. These creeks range in size from trickles that grow fat brookies and cutthroats to small rivers that harbor huge browns and rainbows.

At twilight of a summer day, I stumbled on a spring fishery of fabulous promise. While traveling down from high country, I noted this meandering stream next to the road and questioned a resident rancher.

"Any fishing.?"

"Lots of trout in Bluewater Creek." Then he winked, "You wouldn't be afraid of rattlesnakes?"

"Damned respectful."

"Lots of them, too," he cackled.

I entered the stream within a tangle of briar and brush, stepping softly through silt rubble as I edged towards a string of rises at a bend. I flicked some rolling casts gently and dropped the fly above four active trout.

The quiet movements of the line never spooked the preoccupied fish, feeding all too blithely around the drift of the dry fly. The trout rose in a deceptively patient manner, tight against the outside rim of the bank. Tails breaking in the air and snouts poking through the surface belatedly disclosed the immense proportions of the fish.

In moments of increasing quandry, I hastily changed fly patterns and lengthened leader tippets. Each futile testing of a fly wasted precious bits of time in the quickly darkening tunnel of trees. The frustrating selectivity of the feeding trout remained a baffling mystery.

The mistake lay in hasty angling not to take some minutes to seine the slow current to discover the primary item of feed; the rash flailing had only obscured the solution to a specific feeding problem.

In the dark I clawed through the thorny brush, threading

26

among sinuous-appearing black sticks littering the rocks, ever alert for the warning buzz of a rattlesnake, but more immediately beleaguered by ravenous clouds of mosquitoes.

On a freestone stream, the character of the habitat diminishes the issue of selectivity. For a scanty emergence of aquatic insects, a general imitation fools the trout. During any heavy fall of insects, the fast water still harbors non-selective feeders.

But insects of an alkaline spring creek appear in dependable plethora, even minute forms collecting on the water in regular abundance; more than a single type of fare often joins in multiple profusion to cause individual trout to concentrate on a particular insect in total disregard of other available food.

The reason for selectivity in this preference for a specific insect narrows to a simple equation:*

$$\frac{\text{Abundance of feed item X Bulk of feed item}}{\text{Difficulty of capture}} = \begin{array}{c}\text{Energy spent}\\ \text{per calorie}\\ \text{consumed}\end{array}$$

In the quest for ample food, a trout lives in fine balance between calories consumed and calories expended. Economy of motion is a necessity of existence for a feeding fish. In a slow water environment, the trout sips at leisure even on minute fare, with an efficiency gained through selection of a single item.

Selectivity is strengthened further because, without the ability to judge each passing bit, the trout only accepts a fraud corresponding to the natural. The emergence of a number of insects soon establishes a rhythm of feeding based on sight identity.

---

*This equation was presented in an article by the author that appeared in the May/June 1972 issue of Fly Fisherman Magazine.

The professional fly fishermen of France — the suppliers of table trout for hotels and restaurants — handle the problem of selectivity uniquely. On spring-flows with wild brown trout, these practical disciples of profit avoid the frill of matching any predominant feed-item.

The angler places a basic Partridge Hackle pattern up and across in a curving shepherd's crook cast. He drops the fly at a critical distance (approximately 4 inches) away from the back and side of the eye of the trout, measuring the delicate fall to coincide with the rise-rhythm.

Proper execution usually fools the fish into immediate no-inspection acceptance, but the technique is no easy feat. It requires a keen eye to mark the exact holding position of a trout, and even with perfect execution of the cast, the method sometimes fails to trigger a strike.

I explained the ploy to Henry Landers and Early Crotty, "Sometimes, when nothing else works, this is a last-chance shot for me. I don't do it enough to be really sharp, but it's nabbed a few 'untouchables.'"

"Try that on Faithless." Landers praised a particularly canny trout in Hot Creek, "He snubs everything."

The desert spread in boulder-jumbled sagebrush patches on the eastern slope of the Sierra Mountains. Dry-wash gullies cut from canyons to spill in mud-flat alluvial fans. No moisture pocked the white stains of alkali depressions.

After the long drive, the view of Hot Creek burst as an anomaly of chilled water in a parched setting. "It's beautiful."

At the house we pumped hands in a general introduction — Roy Moore, Mel Lakeman, Simon Dodd, John Demaree, George Birdsell. "If you're ready, we'll start on Faithless."

"That's your fish, Henry."

"He's a ritual of initiation."

As we hiked the bank of the crystal flow, each fisherman related a story of the trout. "One time, on a perfect drift, he just lay there under the surface, sliding back with the fly — 4 feet, 6 feet, 8 feet — and there I am, leaning out to fight the drag. I just ripped the line off the water, because I wasn't going to fall in just to make him laugh any harder."

This trout huddled flush beside a jut of rock, lazing in an intricate jig-saw of squiggling currents. Any natural insect filtering with the flow reached the fish in a gliding sideways skid. The water broke into three narrow bands of varying velocity, with the trout snug in the two foot width of the center lane.

The anglers spread back in a wide semi-circle and proffered some last minute advice. "You know, don't you," Henry needled, "that you don't pass the initiation if you catch the fish."

"Then everyone passes the initiation," someone laughed.

When I lengthened the line the first time for the curve cast upstream, choosing a "win or lose" gamble to end this spectacle, the number 20 Grouse Hackle dropped beside the eye of the fish. At the feeble concussion of the fly, the trout whirled in a blind spin to snatch the fake.

While I pressured the rambunctious 19-inch rainbow, the group hunched with pursed lips and shifting feet in an effort to speak through passing smiles. "Nice"; "Real good"; "Knocked him."

After I released the infamous fish, I insisted, "That was dumb lucky."

"We wanted you to catch him. Really we did — we were rooting for you," Henry shrugged. "It's just that we didn't want you to make it look so easy."

I recouped a position as an amiable associate only minutes later, when I snagged a backcast in the lone scraggly tree of the canyon. "This is a tough stream," the members offered in solicitous gratitude, a climber scrambling for the tangled fly, "with these brushy banks."

The art of fly fishing is inextricably wedded to spring-water creeks. The historic advances of technique and imitation link

29

tightly with these demanding waters, which spawn problem situations. The challenge of bitter refusals fosters solutions that apply to gentle-water habitats everywhere.

Selectivity ranks high on these rich spring flows — 60% or more rises on a rich alkaline flow, versus 15% rises on a freestone chop. The pampered trout structure their feeding on a trigger-characteristic of the natural.

Devotees of these creeks cherish moments of fuss-time angling for the challenge offered by each individual trout. The entire quest for a hyper-selective fish raises the value of fly fishing above any mere attainment of catch.

Bill Seeples

Chapter 4

The Lure of a Mountain Lake

Even in late April, winter lingered in the region. The valley town lay blanketed with grey-bitter clouds that tumbled in thick procession. A gusty bluster of wind was pocked with passing spits of snow. Spring seemed far distant, and only leaf buds swelling on water-edge willows promised any seasonal change.

Howard Thompson puttered in his shop with an array of cameras. He cleared the equipment, displaying his usual willingness to divulge the angling gossip of the area. "That big grey nymph is working in the river."

He pointed to a rusting coffee can on the shelf, where fat larvae of the Orange Dancer cranefly *(Tipula)* wriggled in the water. The specimens were models for the matching flies he created to cast the river. The weighted patterns, drifted deep, caught trout in the Clark Fork all winter.

But now I desired an angling different from the nymphing

31

game. "Are any ponds opened up yet?"

Bustling people strode on the main street, wearing hats and mufflers drawn against the early chill. "We might find some fish cruising the shallows."

"I need a change of scenery."

Momentarily in the afternoon the sky cleared as patches of blue broke the grey cap of sky. But as we drove to the pond, the wind swept off the mountains in a shift to a southerly blow; not cold, but strong in the intermittent lull and push.

The small spring-fed irrigation tank sat in a hollow on the range-land. An unsightly rim of mud circled the water, the result of a draw-down, but the pond lapped ice-free in the bowl. Mats of weeds broken by the current piled in drifts against the windward shore, and a chop of miniature white-caps obscured any sign of feeding fish.

Howard explained the topography of the pond, the bottom con-tours unknown to either Galen Wilkins or me on this first trip. "The original channel is the deepest part, running there from the inlet," he threaded a finger in the air to trace the path, "around the island to this pump block."

I began to fish by slamming out casts with a weighted nymph, using a count-down sink to allow the fly a slow retrieve over the bottom, because I presumed the sluggish trout were lying in the deepest water. For the first half-hour I probed the weed tops of the channel with the methodic hand-twist technique, all the while never feeling so much as a nip on the Damselfly Nymph.

Neither Galen nor Howard caught any trout, but Howard exhi-bited a bright red nymph-like pattern on a No. 6 hook, "I had a solid hit on this one, but it's not quite right;" and in his manner he changed the fly as he sought a "killer" choice.

Over the flats at the far side of the pond swallows flew in weaving lanes, the birds diving to snatch some type of insect over the water. The tattletale bug-chasers gave away a secret hidden in the rough water: there was a hatch in progress.

32

Galen and I decided to walk around the shore. "Are you coming, Howard?"

He snipped the tippet to change to a different fly, "Go ahead."

When I stalked close to the shallow weed beds, I spotted bulging breaks in the surface. I clinched on a dependable Wooly Worm to supply the first trout, because there were no flying insects visible to hint at a matching pattern, and tossed it beyond the patch of swirling trout.

On many of the retrieves, I received feeble hits. Each time, the barb missed a solid bite; or the lip-hooked trout tore free in the vegetation. One Judas-fish mercifully hung solid after the frustrating minutes of botched strikes.

There was no need to kill the 12-inch brown, not with pupae of the black midge jammed in his gullet and gills. A No. 18 artificial, matching a sample of the insect, was fastened to a fined-down tippet.

All of a sudden the fish were no longer difficult to catch. A swirl assured a strike, with the barb seating firmly in the corner of the mouth. Not a single fish slipped free, although I snapped flies off when I set too hard on trout too heavy to be bullied.

As I skidded in an 18 inch brown, I glanced behind and noticed Galen. "Any luck?" I called.

He shrugged, "I've had lots of hits, but I'm missing all of them."

"The same thing was happening to me until I changed to a smaller fly."

He flicked the rod tip, "I should have known it."

"They're taking midge pupae."

Galen hustled back to the dam-site, each step kicking up gobs of mud. He hollered, "Some real nice fish rolling."

I gazed over at Howard on the cement foundation of the pump; a man more than forty years older, he fished with as much enthusiasm as either of us. "Hey," I shouted, "we're nailing them over here."

I lost any return call in the wind, accepting instead a jaunty wave of acknowledgment. When I glanced over later, I watched him playing a trout, and I assumed he was also matching the predominant black midge.

At twilight the birds deserted the area of the shoals. Rises of the smutting trout dwindled to an occasional sporadic break, until the fish stopped feeding altogether. Casting over the edge of deeper water yielded only random small trout.

I circled the pond to the pump-block, where Howard still indefatigably fished. "Really hot over there," I said.

"It's been good here."

I spotted a trout stretched on the gravel. "That's a nice fish."

"I caught two more just like that one."

I measured the brown at 21 inches. "You know, I wasted a lot of time over there feeling sorry for you." I asked, "Did you get them on a small dark fly?"

He grinned as he showed me a fat orange nymph pattern, "On this."

I shook my head. "You just ruined a good theory about selective fish." I stared at the traitorous lunker for a moment and then offered, "Mind if I clean him?"

I gutted the trout by carefully slitting the stomach wall, squeezing out a jam of orange scud, the angler's "freshwater shrimp," and separating this *Gammarus* scud from bits of weed debris. "I guess they were selective on this side, too."

Galen returned to report his experiences on the far rim of the pond, "I got a nice brown on a small Hare's Ear."

After I finished scraping the body cavity, I hefted the large trout. "Howard got this one over here, and two other big ones, while we were chasing the dandy prats."

That day Howard had solved an angling problem through an empirical approach. In meticulous fashion he tested patterns and retrieves, narrowing the choices after the increased success of each variable, a method predicated on a profound respect for the vagaries of trout fishing.

Lake fish often display a fussy temperament. The proper fly or the correct technique falls into a specific category. When all else fails to interest these trout, which function with habitual punctuality, it is the manner of presentation that often determines the response to a fly.

Certainly, an angler encounters moments of plenty on the lakes; and equally as sure, he experiences occasions of complete befuddlement with wilderness trout. Lake fish are as fickle as any "experienced" brethren of the stream. The reasons for the trout's selective bent, often unfigurable even to a knowledgeable devotee of still-water habitats, are linked inextricably to circumstances of the environment.

As a defense against totally blank moments, a fly fisherman gathers a repertoire of odd techniques. The high-country angler collects a "bag of tricks" after his experiences of frustration, finally adopting a philosophy of versatility, an "anything" approach; he wisely admits to not knowing the reason for obstinate behavior of trout — and then stops relying on totally reasonable methods.

In Connecticut, during an evening with Joe Garman, the angling discussion centered on problems of lake fishing. The story-swapping grew especially illuminating because of Joe's extensive experience on lakes from Maine to Labrador.

Joe popped a new wrinkle with a trick different from any in my assortment of chance solutions to periods of desperation fly fishing. "From a boat there's a technique that works with a Hi-density line. Take a slow sinking Muddler Minnow and cast it in towards the shore-edge that drops off sharply. Let the line belly down to the bottom, then stick the rod tip into the water and retrieve with quick jerking snaps, making the fly dive down the incline."

I jotted a description of this method in my fishing notebook and added a reference to steep-walled crevice lakes of the mountains, "I know a few problem spots where this might work."

The technique varied in important ways from the popular

"damselfly retrieve" of Henry's Lake. Although the dart of the fly and the thrust of the rod into the water paralleled the manner of covering spring-holes, the diving descent of the sink-head pattern created a different illusion of imitation from the deep level stutter of the Damselfly Nymph.

A series of specific simulations of the leech fit the slow-sink requirement of this method. In the predominant grey and red colors of these lake invertebrates, a feather and hair softness copies the undulating motion of the natural swim. A radical top- and bottom-trimmed head of buoyant deer hair alters the sink rate.

RAINBOW LAKE LEECH

Hook: Mustad-Limerick 3123 (regular length shank); 4, 6,
Thread: 2/0 grey nylon
Body: Dark red marabou fibers (twisted on the tying thread into a rope)
Rib: fine copper wire
Under Wing: Dark grey marabou fibers (tied only slightly longer than the hook)
Over Feather: 1 grizzly saddle hackle dyed a scarlet red (tied flat over the marabou wing — slightly longer)
Head: Natural grey deer hair (spun — clipped short top and bottom to leave a thin planing collar in a V along the sides)

More than two years later, in dappled shallows of water, I toyed with a natural leech on the tip of the fly rod to study the movements, dragging the animal away from a crevice of rocks. Each time I exposed the leech, it turned immediately towards the bottom.

Jimmy Burns and I flogged Rainbow Lake during the bright day. We gawked at 20- to 30-inch trout that cruised at the break separating the deep water from the shelf. We sank flies of various design to the noses of the fish.

"You're not going to catch any trout sitting there," Jimmy

offered.

"I'm trying to think of something else to do."

"You didn't believe me," he laughed. "Well, did you ever see so many big fish that no one can catch?"

"No," I admitted.

"Every once in a while one of them gets hungry. I caught only three fish here last year, but they were all over 4 pounds."

The special leech imitations remained forgotten in the box, until I remembered the technique of the diving fly. I snipped off a standard marabou leech-pattern and tied on the hair-head creation. I changed the sink-tip line for the full Hi-d type.

Jimmy watched me paddle in a tube-float onto the lake, "Another big idea?"

"It probably won't work any better than the others."

"You just come back here," he advised. "Hard work will make the difference, not any fancy trick."

After I plopped the leech pattern over the edge of the shoal, I allowed the belly of the line to drop for a count of ten. On repeated casts I extended the time to a 22 second fall, until the fly tapped the rock boulders on the sloping retrieve.

During moments of casting blind, I doubted the effectiveness of the technique. Then, as the fly wobbled and spurted on another retrieve, I noticed a cruising trout intercepting the path of descent, and I jiggled the leech in an enticing mimic of the natural.

When the fish spotted the fly, it rushed forward to pile into the fraud. It shifted from a lethargic idling to rash attack, the flank of the rainbow reflecting a burnished silver as it twisted to grasp the hook sideways in the mouth.

"That's the way," Jimmy ran along the rocks, "You finally got lucky."

I finned the tube backwards to play the heavy fish in deeper water. "He'll scale four pounds."

Those grey-backed trout proved difficult to sight soon enough to cast to cruising individuals. After another forty minutes, a drop of the leech pattern coincided with the passage of a fish. This rainbow reacted with similar haste to nail the free-swimming fly.

Jimmy asked with a suspicious propriety, "Are you doing something different?"

"Working hard — real hard. Harder than I've ever worked before."

Spires of tree shadows crept onto the lake. Contrasting bars of intensity confused the light's penetration into the water, and the jumble of boulders on the bottom broke the background pattern to further obscure the shapes of approaching trout.

I coached Jimmy in the technique. "I can't see any fish," he said, "but I'll know what to do next time."

I barely glimpsed a form crossing over a patch of pale silt. After I lost the outline of the fish, I held back the cast in an estimate of the swim. I slammed the fly out, but I was certain, during the interminable sink of the line, that the trout had passed the Leech.

On the haphazard retrieve the line pitched suddenly downward. "Jimmy," I vouched, "this one really is luck."

He maneuvered to the gravel beach to help net the 24 inch trout, a third fish over 4 pounds. "Are you keeping it?"

"Not this time."

He revived the rainbow. "There're not so many big ones here now. Fools with dynamite and poison hit it every few years."

"Dynamite? That's a 'Montana Spinner.' "

He pushed off the trout. "The lake is too easy to get to."

As we walked on the short spur-trail down to the dirt road, we crushed sprigs of wild mint to release a pungent aroma, and we praised both the blessing of an accessible bounty-water so near Deer Lodge and the difficult nature of the trout. "I embraced that 'work ethic,' " I explained, "when I remembered the wise words of a 'Puritan' in Connecticut; thank Joe Garman for this one."

Trout of the high-mountain country are practical creatures — any whims usually tailor to the actions of aquatic prey-items of the

38

environment. As fish gather at points where feed concentrates, adjacent spots of water stand nearly barren of trout because they are virtually barren of vulnerable fare.*

A rough classification divides the insects into two groupings: drift fare and active fare. Trout congregate in distinct areas of a lake to feed upon either type, preference switching according to the relative abundance of each.

Swimming and crawling forms of life inhabit shallow areas of a lake. Among the weed beds of reefs and edges, active insect and scud populations flourish in regions of photosynthetic production. Deep waters contain little of the total percentage of invertebrate animals.

But the drift fare items depend upon no particular characteristic of underwater structure. Suspended in the surface film, non-locomotive insects, midge pupae and fallen terrestrials, move with the top currents generated by wind. Stranded refuse piles in a narrow band of flotsam against the shore, and the collection of mired feed causes trout to abandon the prime scrounging areas of shallow littoral margins, to stack within inches of the windward land.

During a day on Boulder Lake, the angling depended upon identifying the migrations of fish. In the afternoon, large cutthroat shifted from the bank to the reef. Then, with evening dimness, the trout gathered at the mouth of an inlet stream.

Early in the morning, I clambered behind Greg Young over a hard-scrabble path. We climbed over the drainage crest to drop down to mosquito-ridden bog lands, on the way passing lingering patches of snow in rock crevices above timber line.

At the outlet-currents of the lake, stones of the shelf were draped with a lush thickness of blackfly larvae and case-making caddis larvae. For a convenient holding sanctuary, the bottom dropped away sharply in a jumble of boulders.

———

*A fine book of reference for the angler preparing to explore the high country is *Fly Fishing for Backpackers*, by Ron Cordes.

39

Oddly, the rich pan of flow stood visibly devoid of feeding trout. Casts beyond the drop point with sunk-nymph patterns failed to draw any follows, although the fanning clockwise coverage of slow retrieves thoroughly plumbed the worthy area.

From across the lake Greg called, "I just missed one right at my feet."

After more minutes of futile casting over the shelf, I left to find the secret of the far shore. Traipsing along the path, I stopped periodically to toss exploring reaches. I waded out to climb up on a rock.

"Any more fish?" I asked hopefully.

"A few small ones," Greg said, "but that other one was about 16 inches."

We both forced casts into the breast of the wind, powering flies onto the lake. Each experimented with the differing rates and depths of retrieve. Except for the taps of small trout and a lost 10-inch cutthroat, we never struck the lode of large fish.

The blow died to an infrequent lull. The water smoothed into a flat sheet, exposing the bottom stones and disclosing ghost-shapes of cruising trout. In clear view, the fish passed along the shallows to sip at the surface.

Twice these cutthroat, in elegant snobbery, sidled past a hand-twist presentation of a fly. The spotted fish tipped in a steady rhythm of feeding and refused to alter their speed of movement to intercept an artificial.

On a premonition rooted in experiences with these cruising brutes, I plopped an unweighted pattern ahead of the fish and allowed the fly to sink with no retrieve in a simple fall slowly past the eye of a wandering trout.

With the take in only inches of water and with nowhere to go, the cutthroat thrashed and churned. "What happened?" Greg yelled.

I netted the 18-inch trout, "That fish at your feet wasn't a fluke."

40

When I sifted the near-water with a collection-seine, the screening was speckled with a thick layer of inert insects, all from a 2-foot wide band of water that traced the wave-line not more than 6 inches from the shore. In the drift were items of different sizes: midge pupae, mayfly spinners, pine moths, true flies, bees, beetles, black ants — but all were similarly wash-fare, with no self-movement.

Across the lake, trout also congregated at the ripple-edge of the leeward side. There, where the wind swept from the trees to touch the water, fish paraded to snatch freshly fallen terrestrials. Spattering the surface with more vigorous rises, cutthroat leaped for moths fluttering with dampened wings.

Along these shallow margins of water, we shared a flurry of 15 to 18-inch trout. We landed nine fish during the melee, all the while hollering in premature celebration of a full-day bonanza as we paced along the bank to probe any minor cove for a trap of the drift fare.

But when the steady wind dissipated to swirling gigs scattering across the lake, the cutthroat deserted the edges. The fish departed as soon as the wave-action dispersed the concentration of wash insects, leaving the shallows empty of brute cutthroat.

We lingered too long, catching only stray small trout, while the decent fish gathered over the reef to splurge on emerging damselfly nymphs. We found the cutthroat again, but there were few minutes remaining before darkness forced a departure from the mountain.

The blank moments offered a sad lesson in the changeable nature of a still-water habitat. The on/off activity of angling occurred with sudden finality; not to adapt to the situation doomed too much effort to silly futility.

The high-country angler enjoys a long season. From the thaw of ice in early spring on low valley seep ponds, the fisherman follows the melt of snow in summer to the pinnacle cirques at 10,000 feet.

The quality of lake fishing is in the quest for an elusive prey. The search involves the same variables as stream fishing — the right fly and the right presentation and the right spot — with much less value in a random chase. More of the environment of a still-water habitat is barren of trout; less of the dietary fare of a lake is haphazard in distribution.

The approach to problems of lake fishing is one of reasoned search, and a meticulous coverage of prime possibilities is the surest method of discovering a successful technique. The solution is more often the result of logical thought than of fortunate guess.

II
THE TECHNIQUE

Chapter 5

Theory of the Dry Fly

THE BROOK was a bawdy bit of seclusion, a brazen speck of ecological morality amidst a cramp of industrial squeeze. It existed unnoticed and unspoiled, hidden as it rumbled deep within the notch of the valley, with the factory and the houses over the ridge blocked from the sight of a preoccupied angler.

A fly drifted in and out of the dapplings of sunlight on the water, the tree limbs a canopy overhead spreading a lattice of shade. The white-fronting hackle of a No. 16 Brown Bivisible stood out clearly, the pattern dancing on small eddies and pirouetting over miniature falls. A 12-inch brookie, a veritable trophy specimen for the unstocked Connecticut stream, jumped with the strike and drowned the fly on the miss. "You fool," I muttered at the fish.

I picked up the cast with a half-roll and flicked the line, the fly barely skirting a hazard of maple branches. I placed the pattern back to the undercut of the pool, and the same pugnacious brookie attacked to slash and turn with the Bivisible snug in the top of the mouth. I snapped up the rod, the fine leader tippet popping; there I stood with a mock grin, a slack line, and no excuse. "You fool," I muttered at myself.

Properly chastened by the bull trout of the tiny flow, although heartened by the hook-up with a wild fish, I knotted a fresh Bivisible to cast to an adjacent upstream pocket. I fanned the wing flows of rock obstructions, those current edges behind a jumble of stones at the head of the pool, and an 11-inch native took the fly on one of the exploratory floats.

The fish bolted in the pocket, streaking from side to side, but it avoided the spikes of root spears. I snatched the tiring trout as it attempted to dart down-current and it flopped on the rock bench. After clipping a bit of the adipose fin, I released the trout into the still water of the pool

This spurt of action had followed close on a full morning of frustrating angling. In the hours of early light, I only watched as trout rose wantonly to my standard upwing patterns, but the fish tipped upwards so slowly in the clear water that often the impatient currents scuttled the fly downstream, sending flustered trout back into hiding in the shade cover of bottom snags.

As I randomly picked through flies, I selected a Bivisible. A subtle variation in the way the fish chased the pattern, with a certain haste to capture the fly, hooked the trout in the twists of the stream current. The fish rushed to intercept the fraud of an insect that dawdled lightly on the water surface.

The Bivisible seemed to be a cure for the lazy rise of the wary trout. It fell gently onto the water with an air-resistant drop, skipping on conflicting currents. It imitated no specific insect, but as it shivered and wobbled high on hackle points it captured an illusion of a living entity and triggered the brook trout into decisive strikes.

I peppered the head flows and pool edges, casting onto wends among the rock walls. If the fly landed in position to float over a likely spot of water, most of the time a fish was ready to strike at the Bivisible, and I line-hauled struggling brookies onto the stones. In

46

the mile of scattered pockets I fished before scrambling out of the valley, I caught sixteen natives, including two more trout at the 11-inch length.

As I fished through the New England summer, I noted moments of effectiveness of such sprightly flies as the Bivisible, Spider, and Variant. Although a high-floating pattern did not simulate the exact body-form of an insect, trout apparently responded to the "tip-toe" impression. The aloof stance of the fly perched on the surface served as a replica that deceived trout both as an attractor covering a blank stream and as an imitator matching a hatch of active insects.

In the history of fly fishing there have been two divergent approaches towards fooling trout into accepting a dry fly as an actual insect. With contrasting reasoning, the artificial fly has evolved into either a flush pattern designed to float *in* the surface film or a hackle pattern designed to float *on* the surface film. Development has scaled both concepts to successful extremes, the no-hackle and the all-hackle, and both styles of dry fly are found in the fly box of a modern angler.

The dry fly as a flush imitation is as old as the practice of "cracking" a wet fly free of excess moisture, thereby momentarily achieving a surface drift. In the evolution of American dry fly angling, a number of theorists have tied flush patterns. E. R. Hewitt, on a stretch of his Neversink River, clipped the hackle top and bottom on a fly to approximate the natural drift of a stone fly. A man named Brush received an early patent on the design of the Parachute fly. E. Hille, in a letter to Ray Bergman published in the 1952 revised edition of *Trout,* described his Emergent Dry Nymph as a hackle-less upwing pattern. Vincent Marinaro, in his classic *Modern Dry Fly Code,* developed surface-level constructions such as the Jassid and Quill-Bodied Spinner to imitate terrestrials and mayflies. Most recently, Doug Swisher and Carl Richards, in *Selective Trout,* expanded the concept of flush patterns by matching

47

no-hackle and para-dun patterns to an extensive range of exact insect counterparts.

The exact-form imitation of the flush pattern is especially valuable on gentle flows, where trout, in a cycle of selective feeding, carefully inspect drifting fare. The fly presents a realistic visual representation of the wings and body of an insect. The upright wings appear initially within a trout's window of vision. The body of the fly sharpens into distinct view as the fish approaches the pattern. The acceptance by a trout of a correctly matching fly is characteristically an assured yet gentle strike, the fish certain that the prostrate image is safely mired in the film.

But there are certain mayflies, caddis flies, stone flies, and terrestrials that do not ride the surface flow sedately. These insects skip, bounce, and flutter on the water, and this motion of the naturals attracts the trout. The required imitation sits lightly on the film, with hackle-points holding hook and body off the surface. The fly, simulating the insect, appears capable of independent movement.

The innovative E. R. Hewitt, originator of the Bivisible and the Skating Spider, speculated that his Neversink Skater was an imitation of a butterfly. He introduced the pattern in an article entitled "Butterfly Fishing," but the fly is often successful on clear water when there are no butterflies in evidence. It is used as an imitation of active insects of all types, suggesting not body form but skittering movement.

Charles Fox devotes an entire chapter in *This Wonderful World of Trout* to the Spider, describing success with the pattern on the Pennsylvania limestone waters of Spring Creek and Penn's Creek. He mentions an incident where a Honey Spider is the only acceptable imitation of the Green Drake spinner *(Ephemera guttulata)*. The female spinner of this species dances and dips to the water as it lays its eggs, and trout seek the full bodies of dipping females rather than the empty husks of dead insects drifting on the surface. The skate of the Spider approximates the motion of the live insect, and

48

the advice from Fox is precious fact for deceiving selective trout that gorge on this large eastern mayfly.*

The Spider is also dramatically explosive at times when there are no distinctly visible insects on the water. Used as an attractor, as a drumming fly, it stirs trout to rise to the surface. When the midday sunshine of summer drives trout to sheltered niches in the stream, and standard patterns are ineffective in arousing the somnolent fish, the Spider is a final resort of the dry-fly purist. Fished either with a dead drift or a skate retrieve on still-water patches, the Spider draws the "curiosity attack" of trout, and it provides action during an otherwise slack period of the day.

The Battenkill of Vermont, a river famous for finicky brown trout, possesses a justifiable reputation for educated trout, but the meager rainfall in the spring of 1971 left all New England rivers low by early fall. The trout promised to be particularly unsusceptible to any fraud of a fly.

Fred Rapp and I spent most of a morning driving north from Connecticut, and as we crossed into Vermont and approached the town of Manchester, the river flowed parallel to the highway. We parked every few miles to lean at the guardrail and search the river for signs of fish. On this windless day the Battenkill meandered in limpid stretches of clear flow, a surface glaze reflecting the beat of a high sun, and we viewed long flats of water undisturbed by feeding trout.

We intended to check with local anglers, seeking information about the river, but we dallied, and each stop stretched to minutes as we decided whether or not to break out our rods. I coaxed Fred back into the truck, "We'll come back to hit the evening hatch."

I drove, with Fred forebearing nicely until he spotted a small stream entering the river. "Let's take a look. The water might be

_____

*Two other anglers chronicled as devotees of the Spider in their books are Jack Atherton, in *The Fly and the Fish;* and Arnold Gingrich, in *The Well-Tempered Angler.*

49

moving there."

We strung the rods and scrambled down the embankment. With a final stalk we approached the river, scanning the water where the brook mouth bubbled into a circular bowl of an inlet. At a wrinkling of current near the curve of the bank I spotted an erratic succession of dimpling rings. I pointed out the rises to Fred. "Brookies?"

"Maybe."

I dabbed the fur body of a Black Ant with floatant, casting the fly so that it washed against the grass. Fish continued to rise undisturbed, but the pattern passed untouched. "I thought an ant would do it. I was left to conclude that the Battenkill was obviously tough on classroom theory.

I offered the casting position to Fred, noticing the Badger Spider fastened to his leader tippet. As he cast to the risers, the large hackle-fly presented a garish show on the quiet water, but Fred, a consummate realist prey to few whims, chose the No. 14 Spider because of its ability to tempt trout.

The fly completed a short dead-drift float. As the leader dragged and tugged, the hackle curl cocked upright and jiggled over split bands of varying current. The wake of a pursuing fish arched from the cut of grass as the largest trout I saw in over a year in the East wallowed and missed the hopping Spider. The trout swirled to loop back for a repeat assault and engulfed the fly.

The trout panicked in the shallow water, whipping the surface into a froth as it flopped in a single spot. Too big to clear the water, it slashed and slapped partly in the river and partly in the air, the head and tail bending in tandem to throw splashes with each unfolding. The trout flurried in the circle of the inlet, until it dug nose down to the depth of the "bay."

"Look out," Fred warned.

The trout burst out into the river, peeling off line. Fred chased along the shore to gain a spot below the fish, using the river current to help with the fight. He pressured the fish, and it whirled on the surface. "He has to be a brown," he said.

"Splashy brown."

"This big, he has to be."

The trout attempted to slide into the deeper water to sulk, but all his bulling strength had been wasted on the early commotion. Fred snubbed each run, until the fish lay exhausted at the bank. With a two-hand scoop, Fred lifted his catch onto the grass. On a hand scale he weighed the brown trout, the marker jiggling at the 4-pound mark.

He handed me the Badger Spider and I stashed it carefully in my box, saving the same fly to use successfully on difficult trout in Montana. The pattern proved its value as a prospecting fly on the flats of the Clark Fork above Missoula a year later as it nabbed 14 to 18-inch rainbows and browns.

"It's the crazy movement that makes the fish hit," Fred added.

I use the Bivisible on bubbling runs, where the bushy imprint of hackle fibers is visible to the fish, and I use the Spider on flat patches, where the skittering movement of the fly is exciting to the trout. But I cast the Variant any place where the subtle lightness of the pattern effects a match for active mayflies.

In his work on American angling entomology, *A Book of Trout Flies,* Preston Jennings credited Dr. William Baigent of Yorkshire, England, with the conceptual design of the Variant pattern. Mr Jennings used the Variant on the trout streams of the Catskills, and in his book he reasoned on the success of the fly type, "Flies, either naturals or artificials, floating on the surface of the water, indent the surface film because of their weight and these dents collect light in much the same manner a lens does. The trout sees the sparkles of light radiating from the dents in the surface film, and if the pattern of dents looks as though it might be a fly, the reflexes are stimulated and a rise results...the impulse to investigate is stimulated long before the fly arrives within the limits of the trout's direct vision."

Mayflies emerge differently, varying in manner with each

species. They hatch from different water types and from different stages: some pop into the air almost instantly, some struggle tangled in the nymphal shuck, some flutter and dance on the water in attempts to become airborne. The action of the insect leaves a distinctive imprint on the surface film for an artificial fly to match.

Mayflies of the genus *Stenonema* (Light Cahill) are examples of active surface insects with distinctive habits. The nymphs are fast-water clingers, hanging in the riffle clutter of trout streams; they migrate towards the shore line from the edges of swifter water as they prepare to emerge. Rising to the surface, they struggle in the nymphal shuck and drift in the film. As straw-colored debutantes slip free of the shell, they flutter on the stream in the new dress of the dun. They ride bounces of the edge flow, hopping in premature lifts to fan their wings dry, skipping across current lanes as they fall back to the water.

The Amawalk Outlet is a stream suited to the clinging *Stenonema* nymph. The stream's pure, chilled water delivers dissolved oxygen, and the quartz and feldspar gravel-mix provides an interstice habitat. The duns emerge from late May through late June, sliding from the heads of riffles down to the quieter currents of pools.

The Outlet is a rarity for an accessible flow: within the shadow of New York City, it exists as a quality trout fishery. The water draws from the depths of a reservoir in controlled release. The stable ecosystem is rich in aquatic life that feeds a stock of acclimated trout. It is a "fly-only" stream regulated for limited kill, where the fish develop a keen wariness after a flux of anglers pound the water in early season.

The sky was cloudy when we arrived, hinting of drizzling showers that linger into the summer months. As we hurried to ready our tackle, rain started to fall on tree tops. As we walked through the forest, water dripped slowly through the leaves to fall in the first intermittent sprinkling of the day.

In the early morning there were no insects hatching or flying, so I clinched on a small Muddler. I finagled and manipulated the fly in all the ways this versatile pattern can be played, busting out an occasional stray trout from the niches of the bed. Either I waded up to work the fly wallowing downstream, or I waded down to work the fly darting across stream.

We paused at noon to compare notes on the morning's fishing. For anglers John Simms and Graydon Fenn the Amawalk was a new river, but both men were knowledgeable about the cycle of insect life. Graydon caught a fine brown of 15 inches on the deep drift of a Cahill nymph; John lost a similar heavy fish after a prolonged struggle, when the hook tore loose from an almost beaten rainbow.

Fred Rapp and I huddled in the shelter of pine trees to await a hatch, but Graydon and John moved astream to resume their blind probing of the water. In tandem they cast meticulously at a deep sweep against the edge, but they passed out of sight still catchless.

The wind kicked in mean little spits, and the river peaked with licks of white-tipped wavelets as gusts swirled upstream. Rain no longer fell, but drops blew from overhanging trees to spatter the edges of the flow. The water reflected a steel-grey light with maddening glare.

The first specimens of emerging *Stenonema* mayflies hopped the currents of a riffle. A few stragglers popped up to the surface. As more duns drifted free of the shucks to flit across the water, a trout holding snug to a bend of the river splashed to snatch one of the insects.

While I stalked the tail of the chop-water, with all attention on the far side, a fish chugged unconcerned in the downstream pool. I flipped a hasty cast with a perky Cream Variant. I twitched the fly to delay the drag, but the movement of the fly fooled the fish, at 13 inches a much better brown trout than I expected.

A rush of duns flushed from the water to skitter with the wind in a clumsy dance. Frantically the insects beat wings to dry in the damp air. The mayflies bounced in mock attempts to fly only to be

53

tumbled back to the surface by the wind.

Trout grew reckless in a flurry of feeding, spray spattering in drops with the slash of rises. Fish chased mayflies only a few feet away from the casting position, but the drifts of an upstream fly threaded an unhindered path among the active trout.

Fred and I pondered on a fishless moment, "The Variant always works."

"Nothing always works."

Again I attempted my "mistake" of a flutter cast that had bagged the 13-inch brown trout, and this change of tactics busted a husky rainbow into a flopping whirl of turns across the water, the sudden commotion wrenching the fine wire hook straight.

Graydon, hunched in a baggy slicker, returned through the dripping woods, "Nice day for ducks."

I pecked the downstream currents with gentle twitches of a fresh fly. Twice I missed strikes, but finally I hooked solid to a fine brown that bulled deep. After the trout tore through the prime water, I landed the pugnacious fish on a gravel slope.

Fred noted the flurry of action, "What are you using?"

I held up a fresh Variant, "The same fly."

A fish rose again in the pool after a few moments. At an eddy the trout grabbed the duns that swirled on the circle of flow. The tail of the fish splashed into the air with an awkward break that exposed an expanse of spots on the largest visible feeder in the stream.

I crept near enough to dap a short line, the fly curling on the current. A quick tapping on the surface popped the pattern into teasing dashes, the fish breaking from a cruising path to streak towards the fraud.

Fred quizzed skeptically as I played the 18-inch brown, "How come a Variant isn't working for me?"

After observing closely, Graydon tipped the technique, "He's twitching it a little."

I grinned, "I suppose I would have mentioned that after a few more fish."

"Divvy up the extra flies," Fred insisted.

Fred nipped a small rainbow with the "twitch" technique. He nailed a beautiful brown a moment later, timing it nicely as John ambled out of the trees. Fred smiled with a "nothing-to-it-chalance" as he played for his audience. He propped the rod high with two fingers and stirred the fish into a thumping bounce.

As he attempted, in this dramatic pose, to step backwards onto the bank, his foot slipped on a curl of grass, and he slid slowly into the river. With commendable aplomb, while he drifted face down and clawed at the gravel with his free hand, he managed to keep the rod pointed at the fish. He spit water as he bellied onto land.

"Take him now, Fred" I offered. "You have him overconfident."

In sodden disarray, ignoring the rolling hilarity of partners, Fred landed the fine 16-inch brown trout. He released the fish and also returned a quantity of water to the stream by wringing out clothes, emptying waders, and shaking his equipment free of excess drippings.

On his knees, he glanced up from the bank to finally crack a wide smile, "I got the fish, didn't I?"

In a final rush of *Stenonema* emergence just before dark, we spread out along the productive run. We each fished a Variant with a twitch, the fly popping down and across with curving casts. We hooked the frisky trout, shouting in the spirit of communal celebration and losing more than one fish to unwise haste.

High-profile patterns are only part of the crazy-quilt of dry fly types arrayed for a modern fly fisherman. Various modes of dry fly construction — from no-hackle to all-hackle — are a puzzle which the dry fly fisherman continually attempts to piece together. When the attractor patterns are considered, the puzzle becomes a four-block construction, with four broad groupings of choice for the angler.

For selective trout that feed on flush insect prey, the angler might choose a low-profile imitator such as a Sulphur Para-dun; for active trout in riffle water he might choose a low-profile attractor such as a Royal Trude; for selective trout that feed on active insect prey the angler might choose a high-profile imitator such as a Light Ginger Variant; and for inactive trout in still water he might choose a high-profile attractor such as a Badger Skating Spider.

An observant angler matches his fly to a natural insect in color and size, but it is often more critical to match the float characteristic of the fly to habits of the insect. It is the configuration of the fly pressing into the surface film that triggers a trout's impulse to rise. The mirror image of the fly on the water imitates the dominant identifying factor of the insect. By modifying the indentation pattern of the fly he selects to cast, the angler controls the impressionistic representation of the behavior of the insect.

New or re-discovered innovations in fly tying constantly widen the scope of dry fly theory. Leonard Wright's *Fishing the Dry Fly as a Living Insect* advances the direction of imitating insect action. His fly patterns which imitate the downwing caddis not only simulate life by riding off the water on hackle points, but they are designed to be fished with a twitch, a tantalizing moment of movement as the fly enters the vision range of a trout.

Pieces of the dry fly puzzle fit into specific slots meeting the necessity of particular situations. For the angler involved in the problem, seeking an answer to the selective bent of trout or to the attraction urge of trout, the choice of fly pattern is determined by variables of the moment. The high-profile fly, at one corner of the dry fly theory, attracts and imitates by simulating ethereal qualities of an actual insect.

Chapter 6

Approach with the Wet Fly

IDLE HABIT poses a curse for the angler. An unreasoning approach to a changeable trout stream limits the potential to adapt to possibilities. A mechanical simplicity in selecting a fly often proves wrong for a situation that varies each minute.

During late morning, a No. 16 Light Hendrickson dry fly performed prettily on the curling meadow-flats of Deer Creek in Maryland. Abundant rainbows and wily browns accepted the sparse pattern as a match for emerging *Ephemerella* mayflies.

Before approaching the corner water, I replaced a slime-drenched pattern with a fresh sample. I primped the fly, working the hackle with a light application of paste to insure a perky ride on squibbles of the flow.

At the bend, the water tumbled over a natural cross-cribbing of logs, the churning break eddying in the undertow of the fall; and at the tail-lanes of this spiral current, the surface erupted with the humps of porpoising trout.

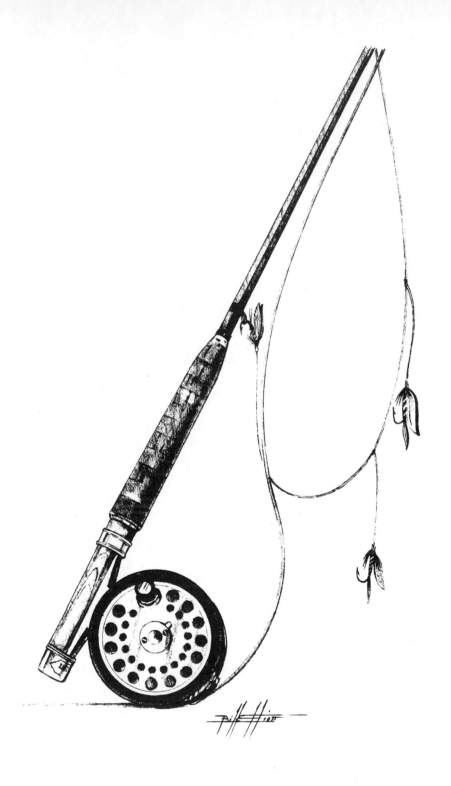

I tossed a dry fly above the fish, letting it pass on a slack leader. For half an hour I cast, while my careful drifts degenerated into a sloppy flailing against the mystery of complete refusals. When a last dry pattern sank to bedraggled dampness, I snatched it hastily from the water.

The heat of afternoon ebbed to a comfortable chill. A mild breeze kicked through the grass with the changing day. The slicks of the stream no longer flowed with scattering rises as the emergence petered to random spats of insects.

"Resting the water?" a passing angler asked.

"Take it," I offered. "I can't do a thing here."

The fly fisherman popped perfect drifts onto a fan of tumbled current in methodic coverage, casting slack-line loops to play the fly in dragless floats. "No trout rising to naturals, either," he shrugged with the futile effort.

"You covered it nicely."

"I fish this water every day," Joe Veach said, "and it never gets any easier."

I squatted near the foot of the cribbing to study the troublesome patch. As I stared at the sucking gurgle of movement, I noticed a jaunty dun ride serenely over the lip of the fall. In the spill-pool, I spotted drowned insects sodden to a bedraggled drift.

I stayed in my hotel room that night tying thin wet flies on light-wire hooks. I lined a row of No. 16 and No. 18 Hendricksons in the clips of a box, honing the hook points of these patterns of promise and pondering a strategy of presentation.

The next day Fred Rapp dropped me off at the stream with a parting jibe, "Some people have to work for a living."

"I have a higher calling."

"And no afternoon meetings."

"Right."

I skipped the intervening water to proceed immediately to the cribbing fall. With a hunched creep to a point below the currents, I scanned for feeding trout, marking two notable fish working steadily high in the drift.

"Resting the spot again?" Joe Veach asked.

"Not this time."

"That's all right. I've already been snubbed by those fish this morning."

I greased the 6X leader to within ten inches of the clinch on the No. 16 wet fly. I crawled belly down and reached a point across from one of the large trout, holding the prepared cast free of the grass. I flipped the pattern side-arm above the hold.

When a fish sucked in the wet fly, I jumped to splash waist-deep upstream of the logs. I slapped the water and reached below the tangle of wood in a desperate maneuver to shy the canny trout from the cribbed maze.

The commotion brought Joe running to assist in netting the 19-inch brown trout. "Beautiful." He laid the fish on the grass.

"That was a bit unfair of me." I sat dripping wet, wearing the grin of a culprit. "Let him go, Joe."

"Did one of them finally get careless?"

"He didn't take a fly on top." I handed over the tiny pattern, "He hit about an inch under the surface."

"A wet fly?" he protested. "This doesn't imitate anything."

"Come here."

We kneeled close to the water to inspect the death-trap of duns, gazing at the crumpled forms of unsuccessful emergers. "Damn," he conceded, "that's what the fly looks like."

Wet fly creations, even the original twelve patterns of Dame Juliana Berners in *Treatyse of Fysshynge wyth an Angle,* achieve an imitative deal. The winged and palmered versions copy common streamside insects. These patterns simulate either drowned adult forms or swimming immature bio-types.

The "classic" down-and-across approach with a wet fly depends on the drag of line to imitate swimming movements of an insect. The

60

precise manipulations, with mends of slack, dampen the pull effect of faster currents.

The art of the wet fly bears on this unseen underwater manipulation that activates a pattern for a specific holding-spot. With subtle motion, the fly breathes against the currents in a sunken flutter that advertises life in the sub-surface environment.

The most futile method with a wet fly is random "chuck and chance it" coverage of the flow. Virtually any technique proves more productive than this flailing "beginner's hope" that scuttles the pattern on unattended swings with an unnatural swim.

Except in the quietest segments of a stream, where an insect might swim faster than the water, an equivalent representation of natural activity stutters the fly in a struggle up or across the flow. The strongest swimming forms avoid the currents, and any aquatic fare trapped in these lanes either advances haltingly or drops unwillingly.

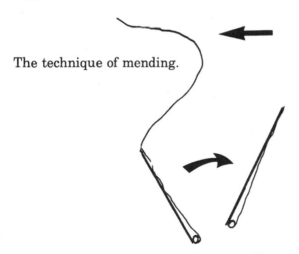

The technique of mending.

Pulling on the line to gather slack to roll upstream is a common mistake of mending. The resulting tension jerks the fly through the water in an unnatural manner. Since no extra line is paid onto the faster intervening flow, the drag is only slightly delayed anyway.

61

The effect of the rod flip.

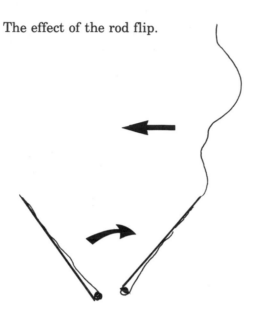

To postpone drag, an angler strips the needed loose loop from the reel, shaking it into the guides. He rolls this excess out with an upstream circle-flip of the rod tip, the arm unbending to reach forward in conjunction with the sideward motion and to push line out towards the drift, thus leaving the fly unmoved in the water.

Mends of line, flipping additional slack upstream on faster bands of current, extend the dead-drift. The fly rides across from the angler, and as soon as the feebly nodding pattern kicks to an uncontrolled rip through the lanes, an immediate mend repeats the seductive natural movement.

When the fly drifts far enough downstream to prevent further line corrections, releases of extra slack from the reel retard the swing-around phase of the cast. The free loops pay out on the water, loosening the sidling pattern into a slow-drop.

A swimming wet fly performs effectively when, with these prime moments of manipulation, it struts through choice trout-water, not by random fortune, but by a concurrence of events staged for the benefit of an expected fish.

In rough estimation, fishing the wet fly, compared to other forms of angling, is the best method for approaching a composite "average" trout stream — at least part of the time:

1. Wet fly (standard) — 15%
2. Pupa (caddis — 15%)
3. Streamer — 5%
4. Dry fly (searching the water) — 5%
5. Dry fly (casting the rise) — 15%
6. Nymph (deep) — 30%
7. Nymph (pre-hatch) — 15%

The figures above add up to the following rough totals:
Active sunk pattern (parts of 1-2-3-6-7) — 35%
Dead-drift sunk pattern (parts of 1-2-3-6-7) — 45%
Surface pattern (parts of 4-5) — 20%*

Moments of wet fly effectiveness occur when trout actively prowl for feed. In the absence of available insects, swimming patterns attract the attention of fish.

Owen Wilson, an ardent student of the history of fly fishing, ventured to Montana specifically to learn the "swimming technique" of the wet fly. "Maybe there are better ways to catch trout," he said, "but the wet fly is what I want to find out about."

"Sometimes it's the best way to fish."

"Not better than the nymph?"

_____

*This admittedly debatable bit of conjecture does not imply that only a certain type of fly will catch trout during the percentage time — only that it will catch fish in an efficient manner during the optimum period.

"It is sometimes."

Samuel "Eldim" Smith chauffeured for the day along the hot-spring bottoms of the river. On the back-ways below Boulder, he jounced the vehicle over the ruts of dirt ranch-roads in precarious skids around a series of sharp corners.

A bull moose barred the full width of the trail, his spatulate antlers waggling with the browsing nod of his head. Ignoring the honking horn, the moose sidled his rump to confront the intrusive noise.

Eldim stretched to pull the Winchester off the gun rack. He poked the barrel out the window and popped a blast into the air. "One of them bad-tempered bulls will bang up a truck sometimes," he explained.

With the repercussion of the shot, the animal flinched into a prancing break a few yards further down the road. The moose turned to eye the vehicle with contemptuous snorts before rumbling into the brush at a leisurely pace.

"He's here all the time," Eldim insisted. "Come hunting season, though, no one will see him. Just as well, maybe. You know Mackey? He snuck out here to poach one summer. Says the beast came running. Mackey says he put one right between its eyes. Moose never flinched, though — never! Went right over Mackey and left him with a busted leg and banged up ribs."

In the morning hours, during a sporadic hatch of pale mayfly duns, Owen and I stalked the mix-water of the Boulder River. He practiced the basics of the mend for control of a swinging fly. As he mastered the tease of the wet pattern, he nailed seven trout from 10 to 15 inches.

"This works," he admitted.

"It's not the best time now for the method."

"Who's complaining?"

Eldim slowly trudged a waist-deep run of water. He looped a weighted nymph straight upstream for short probes of the bottom. At a swirling bowl behind a rock, he nabbed an acrobatic rainbow of

17 inches. He splashed to the shallows to unhook the fish. "Time for lunch?"

"How'd you do?"

"Twenty or so."

As we heated cans of soup over a small sterno-stove, Owen asked Eldim, "Do you agree? Can a wet fly ever outfish a nymph?"

"Sure," he laughed. "I've seen it happen a few times."

"Only at moments," I added.

Patches of high clouds shifted to cut off sunlight. A quilting of shade covered the valley, hastening a seep of premature chill into the mountain day. The water of the river sparkled in the grey glaze of waning afternoon.

Owen refined his across-stream technique as I stressed minor points of presentation. "After the swing, don't let the fly end in shallow water, because a fish won't chase it that far. Step out deeper so that it hangs over a better spot. The two important things about the swing are where it starts and where it finishes."

A fish rushed across to seize the dangling No. 14 Cowdung. With a flurry on the taut line, the trout splashed against the current. It dug head down into the top water, instinctively using the push of flow for the run.

The strike of this 12-inch brown trout signaled a break to a feeding spree — a boom-or-bust aspect of the wet pattern — and the fish started fussing over the "across-stream" slow fluttering drop of mended casts.   .

We met Eldim back at the truck. "It's slowed down for me," he reported. "I only took a few more fish."

During moments in the afternoon, an active wet fly performed better than the touted dead-drift nymph. As a natural attractor the swimming pattern captured an enticing embodiment of color and life. The wet fly, with its dance of motion, triggered reflexive strikes of trout.

To pin an exclusive tag of "attractor" on any pattern is dubious practice. Nature provides such splashes of color, even in the usually subdued underwater world of a river, that an observer is certain the brightest fly contains an effect of realism.

The gaudy Scarlet Ibis is considered primarily a brook trout fly, but during autumn it is a deadly pattern for brown trout of the Upper Clark Fork. Perhaps the success of this bright red jewel is due to the presence of brook trout arrayed in brilliant dress for fall spawning.

Basically a white fly, the Rube Wood is also consistently effective in this river of fickle fish. Neither direct observation nor stomach sampling provides a sound reason for the attraction of the pattern.

In a series of angling experiments, a drab Hare's Ear was placed at different positions on a four-pattern dropper rig. The bright flies on the cast were a Scarlet Ibis, a Rube Wood and an Analomink.

The results of the first evening of fishing were typical, with seventeen brown trout caught, ranging in size from 10 to 18 inches:

Analomink (black and orange)	6
Scarlet Ibis (red)	4
Rube Wood (white)	4
Hare's Ear (brown and gray)	3

It is natural to seek an explanation of these results within a theory of imitation — a prevalent feed-item simulated in action and appearance; yet if a fly type proves successful but fits no such theory, there is still reason for trout accepting the pattern.

The attractor fly is not effective under all conditions, but a bright pattern of the proper size, used with the right technique, constitutes a viable theory of attraction that is missing from the repertoire of the modern fly fisherman — gone, for the most part, with the long rod and the native trout.

Two variables were controlled in the tests to insure the success of bright patterns: the dropper rig was fished with a swimming motion, and the flies were tied on No. 18 hooks. To eliminate the importance of position, patterns were rotated on the leader.

The determining factor of success for the bright fly was a life-like swim action, in a pulse not faster than the current flow. Anything in the environment of the trout swimming across and up advertised itself as alive; the bright coloration only provided high visibility exposing a vulnerable prey.

The "attractor" worked best during periods of slack insect activity. At moments of random selection, trout seemed more willing to chase a curious intruder, roaming the bottom instead of limiting feeding movement to individual current lanes.

Will Eaton once mentioned, when we talked about his favorite trout stream, the Esopus River in New York, "During the flush of the outlet tunnel, a Royal Coachman on a dropper fools some nice browns, but it doesn't work except in high water."

"Try the fly on a No. 18 hook," I suggested.

Will sent a note in August, "When I credit a Royal Coachman wet fly, the fellows don't believe it. They think I'm catching fish on a secret pattern."

The stream passing within two hundred yards of the house was fringed by lofty oak and maple trees. The water rushed in twisting haste over hill-country bedrock. Brook trout waited at the margins of riffles, and brown trout hung in scarce, intermittent pools.

For short stints of angling on this stream, a favorite outfit stayed assembled in a corner in the front pantry. The leader stretched pre-set with a dropper rig (the monofilament pinned on a wall hook to keep a coil from forming), and the wet flies hung from the tippets.

That summer I experimented with this venerable wet fly dropper rig. I suffered from tangled leaders and fouled patterns during fishless moments — all to whet the fanaticism of a diehard mocked by failure — and yet I never doubted the fish-catching prowess of the two wet flies. Even as I fiddled in trial and error to

67

achieve the intricate manipulation, I nabbed stray trout. As I studied to match the swim-action of the patterns to the character of the water, the catch ratio increased with skill.

My experiences revealed fresh secrets each evening. Success with the method required more than a cursory knowledge of the water, because the moment the cast touched the surface; the angler monitored the drift/swim/swing of the flies. The action was not random; it was tailored precisely to fit the prime spots in the stream.

I was tutored in letters by Charles Haspell of northern California, who at the age of 75 still plied rivers with the wet fly technique he had mastered as a boy. "The flies are in the water 100 per cent of the cast, but the moments of effectiveness are limited to the lift at the start of the swing, the swim of the 'almost' natural drift, and the flutter of the drop-back. The line is mended to correct the tension on the flies and extend the time of effective motion.

"How many fly flingers on a stream can mend properly? Watch them some day. Not one in twenty, if even that many. No, because too many think of the dry fly no matter what fly they cast, and with quick air casts they put a line down to let it drift natural for a moment before snatching it into the air again.

"The man shouldn't toss the cast and then strive to achieve an unaffected float. Motion is teased. The wet fly is a managed tool. Because there are few men left to do the method justice, it is dismissed as an arcane instrument."

From the house, the meandering path through back fields intercepted Little River at a bend. A boulder split the flow at this corner, and the force of current swung to the far side to dig into the bank. A slick behind the jutting rock spread over a deeper cut.

In late summer, notable emergences of insects were absent from the freestone water. A few mayfly duns hatched sporadically, or a few stray caddis flies fluttered erratically in the late afternoon. With this paucity of surface fare, the river was suitable "wet fly" water. A dropper-set of two or three wet patterns searched the hidden holding spots of the stream.

In dead water immediately to the rear of the boulder, the drag of faster currents buffeted the line at each side of the obstruction. Only a slack line drifted directly down allowed the sunken patterns to curl with the flow into the lower strata. As the line tightened, the flies began an upward swim in a tantalizing mimic of emerging insects. On the surface the taut line held the flies to skip and tease in imitation of the dance of an egg-laying caddis female.

Preliminary casts to near currents behind the rock either hooked or gently dispersed any culprit trout to flee across to the bank area. The flies were placed up to drift alongside the obstruction, and with minimal tension were allowed to swim with a gentle pulse down the run. The line was mended upstream to permit the patterns to respond naturally.

The prime requisites of depth and shade occurred together at the far side of the center slick. The glory-hole of the entire stream was this undercut of distant bank, where the current washed into tangles of exposed roots. The hollow deepened as the edge curved, a mixing collection of minor eddies gathering in the corner. The biggest fish of the water, brown trout of 12 to 15 inches, hugged the shade of the recess.

The patterns were worked at the bottom level of the cavity. With a "classic" down-and-across cast, the angler threw slack to allow a free sink. As the line bellied with the faster intervening flow, the flies twitched into the start of the swing/rise at a crucial instant of enticement. The dance of the patterns continued only for a moment of effectiveness, until more slack was rolled forward and across to initiate, a few feet farther downstream, a repeat of the swing/rise.

On a cloud-checked evening, in a rare moment for a dub angler, all wet fly movements proved correct. This streak of skill coincided with a spree of feeding trout, resulting in a memorable moment of angling plenty. At the slick behind the rock, the rising flies nabbed a pair of brook trout, one of the fish a dark-colored 12-inch specimen taken on a No. 16 Leadwing Coachman. With the swim-pulse of the

69

drift along the near side of the rock, the No. 14 Light Cahill stretcher hooked two 8-inch brook trout and a 10-inch brown trout. Along the bank cut, the flies tapped a set of decent brown trout of 13 and 14 inches.

The largest fish leaped in splashing thumps as the trailer fly flapped in the air. The rich-spotted holdover battled strongly next to the mid-stream rock, but the trout faded below the heavy water, tiring as it cleared the line free of the boulder.

As the Leadwing Coachman dangled loose in the slow current behind the hooked fish, an audacious brook trout dashed from deep water to nip at the fly. The 6 inch pirate missed the hook, but the startled brown trout bolted to the head of the pool to churn in a final commotion. Then the fish drifted backwards, sliding onto the mud beach.

I cast one more time, skittering the dropper pattern teasingly on the slick behind the rock. I skipped the Leadwing Coachman on the surface until the brook trout attacked the fly. I set the hook and reeled the small protesting fish across the water.

In a series of fine letters, Charles instructed with either praise or admonishment as he answered my accounts of angling experience. "The automobile is the worst thing ever to happen to the fisherman. There's too much of a flit-about habit now. A man bounces from spot to spot even in a single day. As if the secret of success is a magic bit of water and not the technique that is required on any piece of river.*

"Stay on that one stream. Learn it. Know every deviance of current force that might create a fish shelter...and then, the wet fly is effective."

I depended on all the techniques of the fly fishing art — dry fly, nymph, streamer, and wet fly — and I toyed with the myriad aspects

---

*Charles wrote, "Effective? The wet fly was banished from the private chalk-streams of England. Do you think that anyone would bother to ban a method that didn't catch trout."

70

of each specialty to find its specific worth. As I learned the nuances of the wet fly, I discovered its effective moments and perceived that it was not the easiest technique of fly fishing.

The art of the wet fly is a craft reminiscent of earlier fly fishing, when a soft rod achieved the gentle rhythm necessary to cast a team of wet flies and when the multiple cast was fished with a studied intricacy. Pools of holding potential are nit-picked with a patience that binds a fisherman, in this less hurried form of angling, to his home river in close communion.

BLOOD KNOT

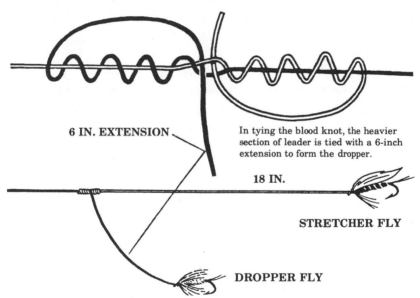

6 IN. EXTENSION

In tying the blood knot, the heavier section of leader is tied with a 6-inch extension to form the dropper.

18 IN.

STRETCHER FLY

DROPPER FLY

Bill Seeples

71

The Wet Fly Leader:

The construction of the leader is critical to the presentation of two or three flies. Using stiff monofilament for all sections, a functional tying formula is:

Attached to the	.018 — 36 in.	.012 — 8 in.
permanent butt	.016 — 28 in.	.010 — 10 in.
section on the line	.014 — 8 in.	.008 — 18 in.

9 ft. long   dropper 2X   stretcher 3X

The casting cycle with the dropper rig is slow, the line forming a wider loop than normal to keep the dangling flies from tangling, and the leader is designed for a slightly slower turn-over than the standard leader.

The dropper tippet is formed by leaving an extension of six inches in the heavier (.010) leader material of the final blood knot. The flies are tied to the tippets with an improved turle, a knot that keeps the head of a fly in line for the proper swimming action.

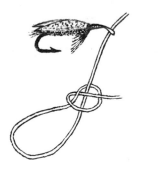

Bill Seeples

72

Chapter 7

The Moment of the Nymph

IN HIS ANGLING NARRATIONS, Ernest Schwiebert fishes a variety of rivers, and his rich language never fails to account for beauty of the land or harshness of the weather, or to include mention of invaluable companions or recognition of historical precedents, because he writes with a poetic conception that instills each of these angling values into the chosen situation.

A copy of *Nymphs* sits on my desk in a worn paper jacket, the cover frayed at the edges not from abuse but from constant usage. Only a few angling works—*Remembrances of Rivers Past* being one of these — attain the allure to require constant rereading. These books singularly bear the responsibility for many pilgrimages to hallowed water.

In *Nymphs,* Schweibert wrote about the Au Sable of Michigan: "...its smooth currents are broken by deadfalls of cedar and pine. It is these tangled deadfalls that are part of its secret, since they

shelter a surprisingly large population of trout, and the rest of the secret is its rich alkalinity — born in the lime-marl bogs and subterranean limestone of the sand-country forest."

He advised: "...[a nymph] would also reach a lot of places impossible with a dry-fly drift."

On the main river, jigsaw limbs of dead trees poked under the surface, their snarled branches protecting any unseen trout. A cast into the web was virtually impossible from a wading position in the middle of the stream, and quick pops that scraped the edges of the shelter only freed small trout.

A procession of canoes posed an even worse annoyance to the angler. Too many pressed between the fisherman and the far bank, disturbing the casting water. Some of the zipping free-boaters veered only slightly to miss a collision.

"I wonder," Vic Pratt shouted, "if I can land one of those jokers on a 4X tippet?"

"It's catch and release," I pointed out.

I retreated to the untrammeled shore and altered my angling tactics, approaching near enough to the sweepers with a stealthy crawl to flip a downstream nymph. On the dead-drift passes into the brambles, I watched for any sudden folding of the line tip.

All the climbing through the stream-side brush, dodging eye-jabbing spears of dead sticks, brought a tacky sweat to mix with the smears of pine pitch. Bees and mosquitoes added to the discomfort of the hot sun.

I lost some of the large fish that buried into the tangle patches, but with a heavy leader I skittered many trout out of the mess. "This reminds me of bass fishing in weeds."

"No finesse," Vic laughed, "but how do you do it?"

"I'm wondering if it's worth the trouble."

To the credit of a downstream nymph, we plucked fish all afternoon from the sweepers. We nabbed trout from deep in the wood mesh, and with bully-tactics pulled free 10 to 18 inch scrappers that otherwise huddled in complete security.

75

Trout too big to budge from the hiding nooks always excited the moans of an angler's dismay, "You should have seen that one."

The dead-drift presentation of a sunken fly proves effective for a full circle of casting angles. The upstream reach with the nymph, the classic manner of approach, fits most angling situations. But downstream and across-stream methods often cover a holding niche in a more precise manner.

At one spot on the Clark Fork River, a slot of deeper water runs straight down from a spring-head. Approach from below becomes impossible due to the sloping drop of the bottom. Only an across-stream drift parades a fly through the entire length of this prime spot.

Neither the downstream nor the upstream cast offers great mystery for setting the hook; in either direction, the sucking draw on a fly transmits a straight-movement response to the line. With the strike at the upstream cast, the line tip pulls vigorously against the current, and with the downstream cast, it drops sharply below the surface.*

At the moment of a strike, the line lying across-stream responds in a significantly different way. The pull does not manifest itself in a directional contact, for when a fish moves a fly the tug transmits "down," and this motion travels only secondarily to the side. The strike-signal shows as a bending of the line tip, or often more simply as a slowing of the drift progress.

Expert nymph technique develops in an angler who possesses a mysterious "sixth sense," the ability to detect a strike that gives no apparent indication, a skill which experienced nymph fishermen display so uncannily. But there actually exists no mystery at all; there comes a tip-off each time at the moment of the take.

The concentrating nymph angler peers at the tip of the floating

---

*A chronic error I encounter in instructing the nymph technique is the failure to stretch any curls perfectly straight in the leader, a crooked bend of nylon masking the power of the strike.

76

line. He lifts the hook when the line does not draw — "nothing" is the critical indication. Not what the line does; but what the line does not do. The angler imagines the path the tip is supposed to follow, including any slight deviance of line-curl or minor change of line-speed and he strikes when that projected movement fails to occur.*

The method of the nymph requires acute concentration. To peer at a moving tip of line for any amount of time, with no missed moments for mental dalliance, demands singular dedication. Mastering the technique justifiably inspires a mild conceit in fanatical hard-core devotees.

The most bandied truism in angling literature is the statement that justifies artificial nymphs: a trout feeds 80% to 90% of the time off sub-surface life forms. This general fact warrants some qualification, because not all of a trout's underwater foraging focuses on the drifting nymph imitated by an unmanipulated artificial.

A slow hand-twist gather of line simulates the migration of emerging stone flies crawling to the shallow edge of a stream. A twitch retrieve imitates the movement of swimming mayfly nymphs darting to the rocks. A gentle lift of the fly represents the rise of emerging mayflies floating to the surface.

The unweighted free-action nymph mainly mimics the immature crawling and clinging forms of mayflies, caddis flies, and stone flies at a moment of uncontrolled drift. The pattern simulates an insect swept in vulnerable helplessness into the faster currents

---

*In a letter, Ken Parkany, a master nymph fisherman, pointed out a significant factor in judging the expected rate of motion: "With respect to the 'infamous' upstream dead-drift method of fishing a nymph, I have a tip; it's one of those things you do without really realizing it and the reason most likely for success. The answer came to me as I sat thinking 'how do you describe' to someone the proper way of fishing this method? The clue is that the line (or line/leader junction that you should be watching) should not be travelling as fast as the surface current. Since the speed of the current is inversely proportional to the depth of the stream (slower at the bottom), it only stands to reason that your line must travel slower than the surface current in order for the fly (nymph) to be travelling at a natural dead-drift speed on or near the stream bottom.

above the dead-water of the bottom.

This drift movement of aquatic invertebrates, which provides the bulk of feed for randomly nymphing trout, acts both to cull the insect population and to redistribute concentrations of aquatic life on a typical freestone stream, where there is a daily shift of 3% of all the free living forms of a water-course.

A trout preys on a dominant species in a stream with general preference rather than with selective choosiness. Often the stomach of a fish contains a homogeneous sampling of different insects that all appear roughly similar in size and color.

On a day of introduction to the upper Brule River of Wisconsin, this facet of nymph activity assumed a major role because of an unexpectedly delayed hatch of *Pseudocloeon* mayflies. Although the duns failed to appear according to schedule, the nymphs nevertheless flushed into the currents of the river.

Gene Rhawn and Denny Nops generously supplied the requisite fly patterns. For the miniscule Blue-Wing Olive emerger, these angler/entomologists recommended a sturdy Comparadun match. They also offered an array of dark-olive nymphs to represent graduated steps of underwater development.

"You guys were kidding about this weather," I waved at the expanse of clear sky.

"We weren't," Gene insisted; "until last week it was a miserable month."

The Brule flowed with only the slightest tinge of color, meandering through cleansing spring-heads and promising rich hatches of mid-day mayflies. In the morning the surface eddies curled past in uninterrupted calm.

Gene poked the sticks of a seine into the riffle gravel. He scooped up rocks to tumble insects into the screening, and then he spread this collection of drift-fare onto the ground. He popped the predominant olive nymphs into a sampling bottle.

All these tiny swimming/crawling mayflies sprouted the budding wing cases that foretold a near emergence. Even in jars, the

78

nymphs scrambled in a restless prehatch motion, rising and falling in foolish trial bobs to the top.

I picked up one of the *Pseudocloeon anoka* specimens. "This is what we're matching?"

"It's the important species right now," Denny explained. "There's another brood that comes out later in the year, but then there's more substantial food on the water."

Without any activity of duns, we chose a pattern to match the nymph. On limp-nylon 7X tippets we pitched these imitations far above any suspected hold. With a leisurely deep-sink of the fly in the gentle flow, we capitalized on a freely pulsing simulation attained only by an unweighted pattern.

When the orange indicator-tube at the line tip ducked in the current, Denny set the hook into an argumentative brown trout. He waded into the river, attempting to move below the fish, but he failed to coax the splashing battler away from the prime casting water.

Another fly fisherman stumped through the pine woods. As he passed, he nodded in a genial manner. "What are you using?"

Gene offered a sample of the No. 24 Blue-Winged Olive Nymph. "We're doing all right with this."

The man pulled on the brim of a felt hat as he frowned. "What do you call that?"

"The scientific name?"

He huffed down the path, not waiting for the full answer. "I call such tiny foolishness a waste of time."

On this stream, busy with early-season anglers, no other patterns turned the fish in a similarly consistent manner. A matching fly for the prevalent insect, or possibly just minutiae nymphs in general, fooled the brown trout better than larger unspecific nymphs.

While we blithely nailed fish on these tiny imitations, Denny grieved over the postponed moment, "There's been a hatch every day in the afternoon."

79

Eventually, with the appearance of emerging mayflies just before dusk, we clinched on those Comparadun dry flies. We revelled in this topping of a day of fine angling, stalking trout at the exact holds that had produced with nymphal patterns.

Nymphing trout feed in several basic ways:
- nosing among rubble to dislodge nymphs — a random acceptance
- taking nymphs at moments of helpless drift — a general preference
- preying on nymphs at periods of emergence — a selective choosiness
- hunting along the bottom for active forms — a general preference

The fish work at specific levels of current where nymphal activity predominates. With economy of effort, the trout concentrate on a particular layer of flow. This habit of feeding makes the depth of the fly critical to a successful presentation of the nymph.

The best moment for the dead-drift technique occurs when trout hug the bottom strata. This period of nymph effectiveness — often successful when all other angling methods fail — lends reputation to the deep presentation.

Even in the middle of winter, an artificial fly offered in proper fashion snatches fish from a clear-water stream. In the mountain states, the technique ranks as popular recreation on year-round open rivers, producing results to equal summer successes.

Not long after moving to Montana from Colorado, a serious fly fisherman came to compare ideas on angling. "Do you ever use a nymph during the winter?" Galen Wilkins asked.

"I've heard of the Colorado method; but no, although I've wanted to try it, I just never have."

"Let's go out next week."

On the rim of mountain, snow accumulated above the valley, but in lower meadows it clung only in scattered patches. The after-

80

noon winds blew warm enough to melt these soot-rotten clumps.

The air temperature rose to 40 degrees of February balminess. "We even have dry fly fishing with good weather," I predicted, "when the snow flies come out. It's fine tippets with small flies to match the little black stoneflies."

But the fickle weather of this mountain climate deemed otherwise. The sky changed from patchy blue to a grey bulk of rolling thunder-heads, the sun disappearing along with the warmth of the afternoon.

When we arrived at the turn-out next to the Little Blackfoot River, the chill dropping the temperature to near freezing and a brisk wind pushing up the stream deterred any flight of *Capnia* snowflies.

I walked along the railroad tracks beside the river, from this high vantage point spotting schools of whitefish and trout twisting in a feeding rhythm over the bottom of the gentle riffles; I noticed only a single surface rise.

Galen trudged along the snow-packed trail. "It looks like a day for nymphs."

"Don't look so happy about it."

I fitted my rod for a dry fly anyway to probe for stray rising trout. With a downwing imitation of the stonefly, I popped casts fruitlessly in drifts over the visible fish, chinking ice from the rod guides and rubbing the ache from benumbed hands, but I hooked only a small whitefish in an hour.

Less than fifty yards downstream Galen tapped an abundance of fish on the bottom. Every few minutes he whooped, "Look at this."

I abandoned my angling momentarily to find a comfortable stump beside the river near my partner. "You understand, of course, that you're not leaving the water today until I get a lesson."

"Come here."

"Let me just watch you for a few minutes."

He covered a riffle with short tosses of no more than thirty feet, gently swinging the rig out rather than casting the weighted leader, and he searched the lanes of drift with these methodical splits of the channel. With each drop of the nymph up and across the flow, he leaned forward to extend the rod. As the fly bounced back down and produced slack, he raised his arms high above his head.

The specialized arrangement, with a long fly rod, consisted of floating line and a 15-foot 5X leader. Individual snippings of lead wire draped at spaced intervals on the monofilament. After the first wrap of lead 18 inches up from the fly, the final two windings on the leader spread 12 inches further apart.

"Ready to try?" Galen asked again.

I fished with his outifit, while he stood behind my shoulder. As I flopped the nymph up-riffle to copy his technique, I listened to his instructions. "Where do I watch for a strike?" I asked.

He always spoke with a relaxed pattern of speech, "Now get that rod up higher."

"How's that?"

"Now keep your eye right on the tip of the line."

With the lead-dressed leader, almost all the rubbed nylon rode beneath the surface. The floating taper-end of line bent upwards in the current; during its passage in front of the casting position, the white tip hung virtually in direct contact with the rod because of the added height of the arm.

After a few late strikes during the initial fifteen minutes, I started to sense the knack of the across-stream nymph, with the necessary pre-judging of estimated line progress, and I began to set the hook on minor interruptions of the drift. Twice I lifted the cast as the fly ticked the bottom, but with the next tap, I solidly barbed a husky 13-inch whitefish on a delicate "touch."

"You're a good teacher," I laughed as I beached my first winter-nymph fish.

Throughout the winter and spring we indulged in fine angling on the local rivers. With radical weighting, we lowered the presentation-level flush to the bottom in the only way to consistently fool fish. We fair-hooked trout, whitefish, and suckers in abundance.

Galen practiced the technique with a fanatic perfectionism. "Now here," he pointed out, "I always soak the lead in vinegar to take off the glare."

A varying amount of wrap on the leader defined the method with artistic exactitude. The arrangement changed with the addition or subtraction of wire for each piece of stream flow. A pinch of weight, determined by water depth and velocity, made the difference between many fish and no fish.

Trout proved easiest of the three fish-types to nail on a nymph. With each take, the line tip slowed to such a visible curl that we announced confidently, even prior to setting the hook, "There's a trout."

The whitefish posed a more difficult proposition. With a subtle suck and ejection, rather than with a "contact grab" of the fly, these fish barely disturbed the progress of the line. The slight draw on the leader-entry only bent the tip into a more narrow candy-cane configuration.

But the suckers represented the ultimate test, a successful hook-up inspiring the "sixth sense" revelation, "I'm not sure why I struck." The tip wavered virtually not at all with the pluck of the pattern — the water only appeared to move a little faster around the line.

The technique of the Colorado-nymph dredged fish from the winter water in the manner of a vacuum cleaner. The bouncing fly scooped everything from the bottom, once the leader attained a correct depth. Each play of a cast through a school of fish produced strikes.

At a pool, I carefully added strips of lead wire after each unsuccessful pass of the pattern. I started to nab fish when the nymph knocked along the rocks — brown trout to 14 inches, whitefish to 14 inches, suckers to 18 inches — and I traded glory-yells with Galen at a downstream riffle.

As a light snow spattered the river in early dusk, we reeled up for the day. We held the rods under our arms and shoved hands deep into pockets. With ruddy cheeks and chapped lips, we hastened towards the car, puffing frosty clouds into the dark, and slid down the icy path of the railroad embankment to our car.

The shock of forgotten cold forced an involuntary shivering. "Get the heater going."

"Damn fine way to spend a winter." The warmth felt comforting on the drive home. "Isn't it?"

"You won't hear me complaining," I agreed.

Skilled imitative presentation of the nymph constitutes the foundation of an all-round fly fisherman. Without basic knowledge of underwater technique, the angler lacks a method that often proves indispensable.

Seldom on a trout stream is there only a single way of fooling fish — at glory-moments any standard ploy succeeds, but during the rare failure of every other method, the dead-drift nymph pattern usually discovers a few willing trout even under the worst conditions.

The weighted fly pokes into niches of a stream with a display of vulnerability. In simulation of a helpless insect, the nymph represents the undeniable charity of the habitat. Delivered so conveniently by the current, the pattern at nose-level appeals to the instincts of the fish.

The ritual of sampling the insect population with a seine serves an invaluable role in fly selection. Collections from riffle gravels or weed growths reveal the imitative importance of specific insects for the particular section of flow.

On many streams the available fare proves not to be the mayfly form represented by the standard pattern, because both caddis fly and stone fly species dominate in seasonal cycles of abundance. It is the different shape and size of these insects that require the specifically matching simulations.

With common-sense observation of aquatic life, along with the angling acumen, the fly fisherman develops the secret of the sunken pattern. The only further "mystery" for success with the technique rests with constant practice on streams of varying structure.

Bill Seeples

Jeff Johnson

85

Chapter 8

The Art of the Minnow-Fly

$\cdot$IN THAT VESTIGE-WILDERNESS of pine forest country, the roots of angling history link with the reputation of the brook trout and the land-locked salmon fishery. Slim-line streamer patterns of the Maine theorists — Herbert Welsh's Jane Craig, Gardner Percy's Adaline, Carry Stevens' Gray Ghost, Bert Quimby's Kennebago — still dominate the pursuit of a foot-hold population of the two species.

"Flies are supposed to be tied for balance," the younger Roland Vinet insisted during the drive through pocket communities. "And that's even more important than their beauty."

"I've never used feather streamers much," I conceded.

Each of the scattered towns consisted mostly of a cramped center street, the main street stores with the framed windows displaying a clutter of sundries in family-name establishments. At the outskirts of the business core, individual two-story white shingle houses edged the old highway, and every twist of road

86

boasted one or more obligatory antique-sale stands.

We browsed through the yard stacks. "Any old fishing equipment?"

"Some."

We prowled even longer among rows of items in an unsuccessful hunt. "Could you find it for us?" I asked again at the house.

The proprietor discovered a deteriorating felt-book of trolling streamers. He pointed out the kinked wire of a twin-hook connection. "No good for fishing, though."

I purchased the memento, the name "Thom. Hagedorn" inscribed on the leather cover. They're just pretty to look at."

We snaked through a maze of side roads before arriving at a single house on the hill. Here we joined people gathered on a screened porch and shook hands with distant blood-relatives.

The elder Roland Vinet showed me to a cabin by the river. "Jay probably won't be here till noon."

"If the fish are hitting," I laughed, "I'm not saving any for him."

"There's breakfast at 7:30."

After the morning klatch, with its mingled chatter of French and English, I wandered down to the river. I studied an expanse of pool, staring with leisurely wonderment that I had never cast a line on the baffling Kennebago.

The river spread disturbingly wide for any pretension of brook trout habitat. Rather than the tiny rivulets associated with this fish, the flow meandered more in a laziness typical of smallmouth bass water.

"Maybe there're trout upstream," I insisted back at the house.

"Try there," Rolin laughed as he sent me back. "Last week Jay caught a 3-pounder right below the cabin.

At mid-morning, near a bow of the river (a long flat called a "logan"), an apparition of a fish burst from the water in a scatter of minnows, the silver salmon crippling a shining bait-fish with this attack.

For an hour trout and salmon humped and swirled in the chase.

88

The fish hounded packs of smelt across the surface, ignoring frantic offers of flies. The spree ceased suddenly just before noon, and the predators disappeared into the deeper water of the channel.

J. Marshall Edmonds greeted me on the bank, "Welcome to a Maine river."

"It's different," I said. "It's a river of fickle fish."

"That's because they're feeding mainly on the smelt," he grinned. "And the fishing gets tricky."

During the afternoon, a thunderstorm forced the minnows against the gravel beach, where rolling washes of water disrupted the bunched fish. Shock waves of electrical booms reverberated in claps, momentarily seeming to disorient the smelt.

Throughout the worst of the storm, trout tore into the schools of bait-fish. "Is there any special way to use these?" I wondered when I accepted an assortment of feather patterns.

"We'll try different retrieves and different flies until we find out what works," Jay said.

Rolling line into the air, we criss-crossed the expanse of the pool merely by letting the wind push the patterns onto the river. Along the rocks we chased bursts of activity and hopefully flopped streamers into each feeding vicinity, ignoring a soaking from the rain shower.

Both Jay and Roland latched onto a succession of brookies, passing my casting position as they traipsed after the tussling fish. "You're moving that fly too slow," Jay advised. "Keep it humping."

I added a skipping speed to the retrieve of the Jane Craig pattern, peeling in hauls of line to keep the streamer hopping just under the surface. On the next reach, I also hooked onto one of the cruising fish.

When it erupted into its initial jump, my partners stopped casting. "Damn if that isn't a salmon," Roland shouted.

"It must be up from the lake," Jay said.

The land-locked salmon fought on the surface, thrashing with powerful twists off the water; even on runs it never sounded to the

89

bottom. The fish simply thumped slack into the line, finally dislodging the hook and splashing arrogantly free.

No one nipped another salmon, but during the blanket of rain we all caught more husky brook trout. We remained on the river till darkness snuffed the feeding action. We reeled in our final casts and walked through the dripping forest.

"A feather-wing fly doesn't look right when it isn't moving," Jay explained. "A bucktail can breathe with life of its own, but a streamer needs the twitch of the rod to make it act like a minnow."

For slow-water portions of trout streams everywhere I saved these patterns. Often on pools of big rivers I took advantage of the slim-line swim of this fly-type, managing to drum up many fussy fish with these same historic Maine streamers.

The swim-action of the pattern ranks as a crucial point of imitation for a streamer/bucktail. With proper selection of materials to enhance the motion-appearance, a fly represents either a fast moving or a slow moving minnow.

The slim-line patterns imitate species — shiners, fallfish, dace — inhabiting open water. On the retrieve, the fly reacts with a quick burst of trim speed. Both the feather-wing and the hair-wing in sparse creations simulate the fast swim of a natural.

As for species that grub the bottom rocks — suckers, sculpins, darters — the blunt-form patterns mimic the clumsy motion of these huggers. A successful copy wallows in a seeming struggle with forces of the current.

These bottom clingers, their drab coloration blending with the strata, depend on concealment for survival. The fish wedge into the crevice-holds of rocks, and with any dislodgment, the exposed prey battle only to regain their hiding nooks.

This motion-index of the blunt-form minnow betrays its degree of vulnerability. Any sustained dash of speed is completely unnatural and deters the interest of trout; but a feeble swim within the dead bottom-flow tabs an easy target for a predator.

90

The crux of survival for open-water minnows rests with their ability for color-change. As light diminishes or increases, the fish adapt to its intensity. An injured or defective individual, without the capacity of color alteration, advertises its weakness.*

Often an opposite-match fly — a darker pattern in bright weather and a lighter pattern for grey weather — proves effective for this reason. The "cripple" representation draws the attention of the trout because it imitates greater opportunity for the predator.

The same ploy fails with a concealment type of bait-species. Color opposition of a fly (unimportant because the bottom minnow models color on the unchangeable shade of stream-bed rocks) lends too much attraction to a slowly retrieved pattern.

Using two bucktails on a leader provides a deadly technique for simulating both slim-line and bulk-form fare. The sparse fly rides on a dropper at least 24 inches above the bottom hook. The other imitation on the tippet dangles behind the opposite-match pattern. At times this tandem coverage performs substantially better than a single offering.

With the retrieve or the drift, one of the patterns always reacts correctly to a particular motion. The leading attractor fly not only picks up fish, but it also induces added strikes for the stretcher. Amid the holds of reluctant feeders, the finder-rig duet stirs the greed of trout.

The basic drift/swim/swing technique of a sunken fly works with either the single or the double presentation, but there are two minor quirks suited to the bucktail that increase the effectiveness of this method. These angling stunts simply extend the deadliness at the start and end of each retrieve cycle.

Tom Thanet and I fished bucktail/streamer flies on desert stretches of the Natches River, pacing opposite banks of arid scrubland and skipping past each other to cover only the prime water of a

---

*Herein lies the explanation for both light (Jane Craig) and dark (Grey Ghost) copies of the smelt of Maine waters.

specific side. We plucked rainbow trout from this Washington stream during a day of no observable insect action.

I cast a double-set with a sparse Black-Nose Dace on the dropper and a stubby Little Rainbow Trout on the tail. With long reaches across the faster middle band of current, I dropped the patterns against some pipe-spires of volcanic rock.

Tom walked on the opposite bluff as my flies fluttered through the slow water of the edge. "Show me that again," he insisted.

"What?"

"Why do your bucktails move upstream when they start?"

With the repetition of the presentation, a fish bolted in from the cover of a rougher riffle to swipe at the jiggling bottom hook. The obliging trout rushed to intercept this fraudulent prop slipping so life-like out towards the dangers of the middle habitat.

On every toss across the stream (the current in this case moving from right-to-left), the sink-tip line hit in a pronounced "Shepherd's Crook." The simple loop placed flies and leader down-flow from the center of the line. When the faster intervening current pulled a belly into the middle section, an initial tug nudged the patterns upwards against the stream's direction.*

Then I laid out a straight line to demonstrate an undesirable effect of drag, a zipping hop that turned the flies immediately down-current, and I alternated straight and hook casts. I failed to draw a strike with the unnatural reaction of a too agile swing on the straight cast.

Along the quiet edge-water, only the twitching upstream jig of the flies excited any fish lurking nearby in the deeper run. The dallying struggle of the two patterns seemingly imitated crippled minnows enough to pose a worthy risk for a trout's foray into shallow water.

"Until you noticed that habit of mine," I admitted, "I wasn't

---

*On the opposite current moving left-to-right, I shift the rod to cast left-handed and still employ the positive curve, rather than the underpowered negative curve, to reach across a faster band of flow.

aware of it."

"Then you do the fishing, and I'll do the thinking for both of us," he laughed.

"Fair enough."

"That little bit of finagling probably means two or three more fish a day."

Tom manipulated the middle portion of the drift/swim/swing technique with artful control. He damped each whipping drag, altering the fly's downstream progress into a slower crossing movement while he kept the swimming pattern in the important broad-side approach. Dropping the bucktail down with the river-motion, he presented the fly in the most visible position to the holds of trout.

I added a final hint for working the bucktail, demonstrating a valuable trick for fishing the swim-cycle of any sunken pattern. "A cheap glass rod has some advantages," I teased my bamboo-loving friend.

When the drag of line grabbed uncontrollably at the flies, I pushed the rod-tip under water. I pressed the shaft in a bend against the gravel, starting a slow upstream retrieve only after letting the cast linger, and I twitched the patterns to return in an unhindered deep crawl.

The stunt prevented the flies from skipping to the top of the fast run. "How does it work?" Tom asked.

I qualified an angling truism: "The problem is not simply keeping the fly in the water — it's keeping it accessible in the water."

These two quirks at the beginning and end of a mended drift control the naturalness of a bucktail. Twitching the fly up the flow or forcing the pattern deep under the surface, keeps the imitation struggling in the manner of a live minnow. These techniques forestall moments of unrealistic action by the bucktail.

There is an effective, although totally graceless, method of probing deep holes scooped by a fall of water. These erosion-bowls are more common now on trout streams because of man's tinkering, often caused by a drop from a road culvert or a plunge over an artificial improvement dam. In natural settings, the holes occur under spill-overs of beaver ponds or under the pool-lips of random log obstructions.

Choice spots are hollowed out during the heavy water of spring. After the currents subside to low summer levels, there are holding areas of relative quiet in the deep basins. At the edges, with a curl-back of the circular drift, or beneath the tumble, with the dissipation of the flume-force, the currents form feeding stations, where stunned prey pass in a conveyed parade.

After casting a sinking line on the tail of white boil, the angler stretches prone at the side of the flume. He then shoves his arm behind the water fall, sticking the fly rod straight down into the hole, retrieving slowly as he feels for pulse and ebb in the revolving churn.

When the fly and line swim below the flow of the caldron into quieter eddies, the pattern plays in prime water, although the sprawling angler presents a totally absurd scene within the supposedly contemplative spirit of fly fishing.

This technique offers a fair opportunity for even a beginning fly fisherman to fool a large trout. The only "knack" of the method is to plan a retrieve-path that allows the current to work the pattern deep through those holding dens. Even the set of the hook at a strike is usually accomplished by line tauntness.

The region is a mecca for the serious fly fisherman, requiring at least one pilgrimage during a lifetime. Within the small town at the west entrance of Yellowstone Park more fine fly shops flourish per capita than possibly anywhere else, with their expert angler/operators: Bud Lilly, Jim Danskin, Pat Barnes, Bob Jacklin; but the clientele stems from a nationwide funnel of fishermen into

94

the area.*

At night the city of West Yellowstone blossoms with a splurge of tinsel and neon into a boom-camp catering to a flush of summer visitors. The country/western lament of loud music issues from each bar, blending in muddled cacophony in the street air. Crowds of tourists straggle on the boardwalk from one cubby-hole to another to purchase trinkets of remembrance.

After sipping beer at a restaurant, we proceeded to Lilly's Trout Shop. We gathered reports of fly fishing on the far-spread waters of the area, and from this information we planned to return to a stretch of the Firehole River.

Galen Wilkins sat in a wicker chair at the reading table. As he spoke with two other anglers, he called me over, "These 'boys' want to go fishing with us."

We shook hands with the introduction: "Al Salter"; "Reitzel Webster."

"We hope you fellows can show us," Al spoke with a lilt of Southern accent, "how to catch a few fish."

"Pot luck," I warned.

Galen spoke in his own West Virginia patter, "They're North Carolina 'boys.' "

Even my Yankee accent acquired an unwilling hint of drawl, "We'll hit the caddis hatch above the Iron Bridge."

The next day, after lingering too long over breakfast, we arrived late on the river. We still dallied as we prepared equipment — all caught in the laziness of the warm splendor — and we even fished the prime water above the bridge in a desultory fashion.

The sun hung too brightly for an optimum caddis flight. The surface of the slicks spread barren of any rises after early morning. Trout held among bunker channels of weed, all but oblivious to any single dry fly 6 feet above; only a few small fish responded to a deep

---

*Indispensable books for any angler fishing this fabulous region are the thought-provoking volumes by Charles Brooks — *Larger Trout for the Western Fly Fisherman* and *The Trout and the Stream.*

bucktail.

In a tortured landscape, alive where most of inanimate nature lies dead, the earth suffered with the gurgle of a mud pot or with the slow boiling pops of clear water holes; with the unexpected spew of hot liquid from mini-geysers or with the acrid stench of sulphur belching from the earth's bowels; with the stained channels of intermittent rivulets of mineral seepage or with smoke puffs of curling steam exhausts.

Al sprawled on the meadow grass while I flogged a wide pool. "We're doing all right, anyway."

When a fish ticked the bucktail, I turned, "There..." — but the trout trailed to slam the fly again with a wallop that snapped the rod down.

"You were napping," he laughed.

"No," I fussed at my foolish lapse, "I was just about to tell you that he hit it once lightly, but I should know enough to be ready on the swing."

Perhaps at lunch Reitzel summed up our lethargic feeling, when he lay back with his head propped against a log. "This is a great town for catching fish and drinking beer and chasing women," he sighed, "but doing all of them at once is like to kill a man."

In the afternoon we shook the doldrums of the day. With a more enthusiastic attack, we nabbed fish in the riffles, all of us battling trout along a stretch of winding meadows. In sight of each other, we hailed the landing of each fish.

As Galen plumbed the tricky currents with a swinging fly, he nailed a frisky trout. He moved along warm-water bogs on a careful trail to follow the fish, picking a path to avoid the caldrons, and at the edge of the river reeds he lifted out a brawny 17-inch brown trout.

In the evening softness the moment promised best for a minnow-type fly, coinciding with a required "I-can-lick-anything" attitude suited to this energetic pursuit, and it promised best for a rapid time-efficient casting that would keep the fly working the

96

water.

Onto each patch of broken current I popped a No. 6 Dark Edson Tiger, flipping this searching fly for long sidling stutter-drifts down the runs, and returning it after every shallow swing. With short methodical drops I hammered the river in retribution for a previously listless performance.

A dozen trout caught during the walk back, charged runners of 12 to 16 inches, matched our earlier results over the entire day. The fish bounced from every niche to chase bucktails with pounces of determination.

I chatted with a passing inquisitive angler. "I'm having good luck with a bucktail."

"I didn't think there were any minnows in this river."

I held up the mottled brown and yellow pattern, "Where there're big trout, there're little ones."

"Basic biology?" he smiled.

A herd of grazing cow and calf elk slowly closed a half-circle around the edge of the river. The scruffy animals, with hanging layers of spring sluff-fur, wandered near enough to prohibit any casting. One bold calf plucked grass within reach of my rod tip.

I carefully threaded through this unconcerned congregation protesting to nobody, "I can't stand fishing in a crowd."

At the parking lot I encountered the general opinion of our southern contingent, "Let's go get a beer."

The feeding preference of a trout shifts abruptly with the 11-inch mark of growth. A big fish concentrates on a piscivorous diet because of the greater bulk of each item, thus improving his gathering efficiency.

Insect fare remains a diet factor even with large fish, but big trout prove less likely to feed helter-skelter in a random plucking that renders small fish so susceptible to capture. A trout of 2 pounds ingests 80% of food-weight in the consumption of forage prey. On streams that lack the major stonefly populations of rich western rivers the average stands higher. Larger insect-gathering trout tend to sip with a selective repetition during prime periods of abundance.

The minnow pattern offers the angler a chance to stalk large solitary fish. The steady use of a bucktail or streamer leads to an average of bigger trout, more middle length 15 to 20-inch specimens, with a reasonable catch-frequency. Except for a particular crusade solely for trophy fish, the general minnow imitation provides the best chance for the fly fisherman to hang a brute trout during broad coverage of the water.

Optimum moments of the streamer peak with the dawn and the dusk time of big trout minnow chasers. In the faint light the fly draws a vicious bang from a cruising fish. Over the shallow flats, the matching pattern simulates the scurrying panic of bait-species.

III
THE NATURAL FEED

Chapter 9

Thoughts on the Caddis

SOMEWHERE IN THE GLOOM a fish chugged with an audible splash. It swirled as it followed insects from a funnel-current below the riffle head. Sucking in a struggling caddis fly, the exuberant feeder broke partially into the air to spread a betraying ripple-wash.

When I cast accurately near this fish, the water bulged and the line twitched — but I missed the strike cleanly. I hustled the next toss, breaking off the pattern in a tangle of dangling willow roots at the undercut. I clinched on a fresh fly after a moment's wait; then, with apparent calm, I bungled another gulping lunge of the trout, which must have been frustrated by this jumping replica of an insect.

I cast once again to the holding position, despite a firm suspicion that the fish now huddled safely in hiding. I brushed the current lane at the bank-edge, sliding floats over the holding spot until the trout burst out to grasp solidly onto the teasing fly.

The fish was no monster, no aged Goliath brown among the pygmies of hatchery fare, but the holdover resident was a chunky 14 inches. The bright female was a beautiful trout for the Sudbury River of Massachusetts.

I released the fish so that it might feed on many summer evenings and possibly live to be a giant for some other angler, to become one of those sly browns that somehow manage to survive the pressure of hordes of fishermen.

In the evening dimness, female caddis rushed in the frenzied moment of egg-laying flight. Into the puffs of breeze, droves of falling insects flopped onto the currents to peel egg-masses against the water. With skips and hops the caddis ran to escape into the air.

Daniel Antonietti sat on a stump, a possible recruit for a network of friends collecting specimens of caddis. He was one of the young angler/entomologists who know each mayfly of the local streams; although many fly fishermen are familiar with the mayflies, only a rare few know the caddis species.

He asked a question as we threaded through the woods, "Why did you start thinking that the caddis are so important?"

"Self-defense," I admitted. "I was getting beaten every time the caddis were on the water. And those times seemed often. One or two small trout caught, when there were plenty of bigger ones rising."

Ruefully Dan nodded, "Like tonight?"

Through the flurry of the brush-hatch Dan caught only two woefully small trout. Fish that keyed on the fluttering action of insects ignored the flawless presentations of standard dry flies. The technique for imitating the emerging dun of the mayfly failed to represent the actions of the Grannom Sedge.

"I need someone to collect adult specimens from trout streams of this area," I explained. "I can't collect immature specimens and raise them in aquariums. I wish I could do that, but there are too many important species that are filter feeders requiring a running flow of water."

We fished adult imitations during the evening flights, but in

102

the mornings we plied new Sparkle patterns that matched the emerging pupae. As we worked occasional slashing rises or probed deeper niches of water, we turned over rainbows and browns — even a rare wild brook trout of 9 inches — in regular procession.

Dan spotted a rise in a scattering spray of drops, but he saw no adult insect that might tip off the manner of the natural. He cast the pupa-artificial across and down, feeding slack until the fly snugged just shy of a protruding rock. He let the pattern lift slowly upwards through the water; and when the line knot twitched, he set the hook firmly into a rambunctious 13-inch rainbow.

He waded to the bank after releasing the trout. "I'm fishing different flies in entirely different ways."

"But they're only different from the way most anglers fish because most anglers don't imitate the caddis."

Dan tapped his forefinger against his eye-glasses in a mannerism that preceded a grin, "You make this research of yours sound like a public service."

"You don't know how noble I've been feeling lately."

"This caddis business is the graduate school of an angler's life?"

"Are you going to help me collect specimens, wise guy?"

"I guess I have to," he shrugged. "Self-defense."

Dan joined a group of friends that eventually totalled 43 fly fishermen spread over every trout area in the country, friends who collected caddis samples from streams and ponds; friends who tested fly patterns on trout.

Dan noted in a letter at the end of that first summer of collecting and patterning specimens, "I can't imagine all the feeding on caddis that I'm seeing, now that I know what I'm looking for."

There is profound blindness of the fly fisherman to activities of the caddis fly. The insects emerge; the insects deposit eggs; and all the while trout gorge; yet a fly fisherman exposed to this glory stares without seeing the phenomena.

On an early summer evening, Galen Wilkins and I stalked

103

meadow stretches, while wind lashed the Henry's Fork of the Snake. Gusts ripped upriver to churn even placid meanders of the stream into inscrutable blank-water wavelets.

"Shall we try nymphs?" Galen asked.

"I'm casting English-style tonight," I insisted puckishly. "If I don't see rises, I don't fish."

As we sat under a tree on a hill, with a dismayed laugh Galen fussed as he exclaimed in his West Virginia twang, "Damn, if this ain't the laziest thing?"

"This breeze will die down pretty soon."

In the air, files of adult caddis streamed overhead in a dense sheet. The insects blanketed so thickly that the cloud-pocked sky dimmed. From the brush, the caddis beat on the wind towards the mating moment over water.

Somewhere down-river out of sight, an angler proclaimed hopefully in a call that carried on the breeze, "Look up there! There's a spinner of the Drake coming down."

"A mayfly?" I wondered. "How can he see a mayfly through all of these caddis?"

That was on the Henry's Fork, a river of famed mayfly hatches patterned faithfully in *Selective Trout,* where educated anglers bantered slickly the scientific names of important *Ephemeroptera* species; where discussions in fly shops harped on expected emergences: "Do you know your bugs? In the morning at nine o'clock, the pale morning dun starts to pop out. And we're waiting for a hatch of the Green Drake to begin any day now."

That was what the fly fishermen on the river had expected to see — "There's a drake," fine preparation usually, but not when a scanty emergence was overshadowed by a blizzard mating fall of an important caddis fly.

In a cove of the river, the wind faded to a twilight stillness. The female insects dove in crash splashes to the water. As the riding or fluttering caddis rode the currents, trout ganged in a sudden feeding spree triggered by the quantity of surface fare.

The dry fly angling bloomed furiously in the remaining minutes of light, the trout hopping on a twitched high-riding pattern jiggling up the current lanes. The thick-shouldered aerobatic rainbow trout of the Henry's Fork greedily accepted any near-imitation of the spotted sedge *(Hydropsyche)*.

From a jut of grassy bank, I skipped and fluttered a fly in an enticing upstream drag as slack line stretched taut on downstream casts. I hooked fish readily on the moving caddis pattern.

A tail-thumping trout rolled to pluck the dry fly, spinning in a quick leap into the air. The 20-inch plus rainbow bent and unfolded to toss the hook with a disdainful shake of its head. It hung for a moment suspended against the back-drop of the sky.

Galen skillfully tracked a cruising fish in shallows of the cove. He whooped as he hooked a mad-jumper, "Look at this one go."

The feeding frenzy ceased at 9:30 p.m. with a sudden departure of adult caddis flies. The glides of the stream twisted dark and empty in fading twilight as we paced the well-worn foot paths of the Railroad Ranch stretch of the river.

I filled in an information card at Osborne Bridge: morning, 11:30 a.m. to 1:30 p.m., 20 trout; evening, 8:00 p.m. to 9:30 p.m., 12· trout; caddis pupa imitation in the morning, caddis adult imitation in the evening; best trout: two rainbows of 21 inches.

The next day in West Yellowstone I spoke with Steve Billeb, "We took your advice. We fished the Henry's Fork."

"How was it?"

"Good with dry flies during the evening."

Steve, an experienced area guide, looked up from a display table. "I don't believe it. I know some real good fly fishermen who were there who couldn't catch a thing."

When Galen strolled over, I told him about the Henry's Fork anglers, "There were some troubles with the caddis fly hatch."

Later we grinned, "Must have been those guys who were looking for mayflies."

But there were other fly fishermen on the stream who had

106

solved the puzzle of the preponderance of spotted sedge. Through careful observation of rise forms, the anglers had marked the feeding rhythms of trout. With patterns conforming to the size and silhouette of a caddis fly, the savvy fishermen had discovered the techniques of enticement.

The initial confusion of fishermen with the caddis fly stems from a basic misunderstanding of its life-cycle. Even with knowledge of the "full-development" (egg/larva/pupa/adult), on a stream the angler often simulates caddis activity with a mismatching pattern-stage.

During the swim/drift emergence of the pupae, trout break the surface in pursuit of the insects in the meniscus. The caddis hesitate in the film until the pupal sheath splits and sluffs from the body. A trout trails the swinging rise of the insect without trying to grab the moving prey, fully expecting the natural to pause at the surface.

During a conversation, Andre Puyans described this feeding bio-rhythm, "Like shooting woodcock — following until the bird hits the top of the swing."

An imitation of the adult caddis during emergence passes in futile rejection. Trout feed either on deep pupae kicking near the bottom or on surface pupae struggling in the meniscus. The slashing rise of the fish indicates follow-through after an attempted capture. Effective patterns for the emergence period are matching imitations of swimming and unsheathing pupae.

The moment for a fluttering imitation arrives with the return of adult insects to the river. The mating flight gathers from hiding nooks of brush, and the female caddis then touch or fall onto the water. The twitched dry fly simulates the motion of escaping insects.

The practice of fluttering a dry fly stands amply recorded in the literature of fly fishing. Since the dry pattern evolved from the hackled wet fly, except for classic no-hackle dry creations like the Hare's Ear and the Blue Dun, the original technique of surface

107

imitation is predicated on a down and across cast.

A detailed description of the calculated twitch technique in *The Practical Fly Fisherman,* by A. J. McClane, proved a boon for a young angler who found drag much easier to control than to avoid on the tight currents of Connecticut trout streams.*

Edward R. Hewitt, in *A Trout and Salmon Fisherman for 75 Years,* wrote: "I myself do not always fish a dry fly by just letting it float with the current. Wherever possible I try to make the fly move on the water, simulating an insect about to rise from the surface. This motion attracts the fish and at the same time it makes little light flashes below the water which a fish may see that would not see the fly itself, just floating by. I find I can often raise far more trout than other fishermen by this method of manipulating the fly. It must not drag, and yet it must move like an insect. ...When the fisherman knows how to work a fly in this way he will get far more fish than he would ever get by simply letting the fly float quietly on the water... I mean simply very slight motions on the surface of the water like an insect about to fly."

In view of historical precedent, the claims of a book-jacket which touted an angling work for describing an "unorthodox method of fishing the dry fly downstream" to represent a "live-insect" through the use of a "twitch" were overstated; but while it was not any great innovation, *Successful Trout Fishing,* by Richard Alden Knight, did stress the application of this technique on Eastern trout streams, with precise explanations of the manipulative method. This book started the revival of the active dry fly.

The recent *Fishing the Dry Fly as a Living Insect,* by Leonard Wright, Jr., includes a worthwhile variation of the wing and hackle floatation of the old Kings River Caddis pattern in a slimmer fly of high-ride design on a light-wire hook. It again describes the twitch technique, but with an emphasis on the fluttering caddis.

---

*As befitting any hero-worshipping boy, I read every printed exploit of A.J. McClane at least twice.

The motion imparted to a dry fly is often crucial for imitating the adult caddis. The slight movement is perpetrated just before the pattern reaches a holding lie. It is an inch-skip that attracts attention to the artificial entering the visual window of a trout.

The difference between an unnatural drag and a life-like twitch is a matter of direction. A fly skittering downstream faster than the current is unnatural; the same fly hopping upstream on the current is life-like. The upstream action reflects a principle of aerodynamics dictating that it is easier for the insect to gain the air with an upstream flutter against the force of water.

The technique of the twitch is easy to execute with a correct fall of the down and across line. The cast is a curve, negative or positive, that curls the fly on the drift. The loop of the leader extends straight above the fly on the same band of current, and when the line is pulled, the pattern hops upstream.

Even during muggy days in September, a diver dons a wet suit for any prolonged submersion in the chill water of a river. The porous rubber traps an insulating moistness which protects the body heat from the cooling flow.

Bill Seeples cinched the straps of the air tanks, "Ready?"

"Let's go."

We sank to the bottom bowl of a pool in the Jefferson River. In a perch of slack water, we awaited the activity of an emergence, a blossoming flux of swimming forms that occurred with the fading of bright afternoon light.

Emerging pupae of the spotted sedge wallowed down a fast riffle and drifted into the pool. Dropping into quieter water, the insects flexed with a pulse towards the surface. In the meniscus, the adults struggled to disentangle themselves from the draping sheath.

A mixed line of rainbows and browns hovered at the lip of the chute, with the brown trout hanging slightly deeper. Each fish sidled with a gentle gathering of kicking pupae. A small trout broke

109

the surface of the pool with pops at near-emergent insects.

We splashed onto the rock beach. Bill fussed with rambling spurts, "No indecision and no hesitation. A trout moved for every pupa. And ignored everything else."

"It's selective feeding to the 'silver ball' of the pupa."

The vexing dilemma of selectivity to the emergent caddis fly posed a problem of imitation. The "trigger-characteristic" of the pupa rested with the silver entrainment of air trapped in its translucent sheath. No tinsel or fur properly simulated the shimmer.

The initial attempt at specific imitation of the caddis pupal-form was an innovation of Edward Sens less than twenty-five years ago. These simulations of two Eastern species, *Rhyacophila lobifera* and *Psilotreta frontalis,* were listed by Ray Ovington in *How to Take Trout on Wet Flies and Nymphs.* The patterns featured wool wraps of palmered dubbing around both an underbody and duck-quill wing slats.

In the comprehensive *Nymphs,* by Ernest Schwiebert, the pupal-type was correlated to an extensive selection of specific species. The author traced the imitations to venerable precedents of soft-hackled wet patterns of North-country English writers, but his flies also included the wings laid back along the sides. However, specific pupal patterns failed to properly imitate the glitter of the sheath of a natural insect for two reasons: the overbody material attained no realistic shimmer, and the quill side-slats masked the body line.

During moments of observation, simple hackle and dubbing English flies easily performed better on selective fish than did more exact representations. The impressionistic soft-hackle patterns suffered fewer obvious refusals from discriminating trout, lacking only a translucent body sparkle and a realistic head silhouette.

I telephoned Bill on a day in February, "Feel like diving today?"

"Not really."

"That's too bad. I'll meet you in a half an hour on the Jefferson."

At the river, while Bill positioned himself fifteen feet downstream, I scattered clumps of a synthetic material. I spread nubs of a new type of Sparkle yarn in the current to shimmer with irradiating reflections of its clear filaments.

Bill popped quickly to the surface. "What is that stuff?"

"It's the material we need for the pupal sheath."

"You won't believe how perfect it looks," he insisted. "I'll scatter it while you dive."

The sparkling yarn, capturing the translucent similarity of the pupa, was a nylon/acrylic material with clear interwoven filaments. Marketed under various brand names — Dazzle, Sparkle, Souffle — it was available in a total array of color.

In our first experimental patterns, some previous fly-tying techniques of pupal imitation detracted from an effective display of the new material. The wing-slats were simply eliminated because in the natural swimming pupa they were obscured inside the air-sack. Also, in a different no-dub sheath construction, a sack of strands was drawn loosely around a true-color underbody, enhancing the "silver ball" quality of the artificial caddis.*

The Sparkle yarn body, a soft fiber hackling, and a marabou-wrap head blended to present an impressionistic reality. Minor alterations of the curvilinear shape increased the effective deep simulation of the caddis pupa.

A different shallow version of an "unsheathing" pupa featured a top-wing of deer hair. This semi-bouyant pattern, with frayed filaments of yarn drooping from the rear, wallowed damp in the surface film and captured the optimum of reflective light.

With results of stream trials from all over the country, comments of early success confirmed the imitative quality of the fly-type. The sparkling pupal pattern solved the problem of imitating the silver air-trap of the natural insect.

---

*An article by the author in the February 1974 Connecticut Fly Fishermen's Association newsletter recounted the initial testing of the Sparkle yarn.
Bill Seeples, tabbing the pattern as the LaFontaine Caddis Pupa, reported the progress of the experiments in "The Effective Caddis Pupa" in the May/June 1974 U.F.T. Roundtable magazine.

To recruit more fly fishermen to a web of devotees of the caddis fly, I toured different areas to offer seminars on methods of fishing the patterns: the dead-drift of the deep pupa, the mended pulse-swing of the swimming pupa, the air-buoyed lift of the rising pupa, the undraping struggle of the transforming pupa.*

Each technique fitted a moment in the complex rise sequence of the natural insect, and each method suited individual feeding preferences of trout. The progression of the emergence determined the selective activity.

Randy Cross asked during a meeting, "The hatch of a pupa? Like this, isn't it?" He slashed the air with an uninterrupted upward curve of his finger. "Just cast the fly and let it swing."

The following morning on a trip to the middle reaches of the Pere Marquette, we paced the river in the brightening dawn, hunting for visible flashes of fish working deep in the runs. For the tandem-angling we shared a single rod rigged with a weighted pupal pattern.

"There's a nice fish," I pointed.

"You take him."

"Go ahead. It's your turn."

"No," Randy insisted. "If we wait for me to catch the next trout this morning, you'll never get a chance."

We parried in a vaudeville comedy-routine of passing the rod back and forth. "These fish aren't taking a pupa swinging in the middle. Cast the fly up with a dead-drift right by his nose."

He pitched the pattern upstream for a sunken pass of the weighted imitation, timing the drop skillfully to coincide with a sideward ramble of the fish. As the brown trout accepted the No. 16 light pupal fly, Randy snugged the line to set the hook.

He beat the hefty 18-inch trout and propped it onto the bole of a cedar stump. "This one was probably taking everything."

---

*These methods are described in other parts of the text: dead-drift in Chapter 7, pulse-swing in Chapter 6; air-buoyed lift in Chapter 2; surface struggle in the Appendix (Emergent Caddis).

112

"I doubt it."

His knife sliced into the body cavity, splitting the wall of the upper stomach and spilling the contents. The pupal form of the *Leptocella* caddis (White Miller) crammed the upper passages of the gullet of the trout.

None of the stream-dwelling caddis pupae, not even the fast emerging Green Caddis *(Rhyacophila)*, burst to the surface in a no-hitch curving rise. After liberation from the mesh grating of the shelter case, the insect drifts with the bottom currents. The swimming pupa lifts through the water with the buoyancy of trapped air, and with strokes of beating legs progresses in a drop rhythm towards the surface. In the meniscus, the caddis sheds its skin with the tensile wash of the flow and pops into the air.*

The feeding rhythm of a trout adjusts with dual selectivity to the sparkling identity and to a specific motion-index of the insect. A fish forages at a specific level of depth, capturing the pupae at the same point of ascent in a repetitive pattern.

In any encounter with an abundance of caddis pupae, successful imitation depends on approximating the routine of predominant activity. A simulating fly intercepts the point at which the fish recognizes the "trigger-characteristic" of the insect and accepts the vulnerable hesitation of its prey. A complete presentation of the pattern — not a mere swipe of the fly through a feeding level — dupes the selective pupal-plucking trout.*

------

*Certain slow water genera crawl to the shallows in an emergence migration.

*The Sparkle patterns, correlated to the individual habits of caddis genera, are presented in the Appendix.

Jeff Johnson

113

Jeff Johnson

Chapter 10

The Life-Cycle of the Mayfly

IN A MEANDER of 14 miles between the settling ponds at Warm Springs, where a precipitation system leeches out metal poisons of the copper mines, and the town of Deer Lodge, a trace sickness of pollution lingers to limit the potential of the Clark Fork as one of the fine brown trout fisheries of the country.

Bubbling surges of alkaline water from the limestone aquifer purify the flow to a livable biosphere. In successive pools dug between willow-scrub banks and ochre cliffs, only brown trout inhabit the river. On rare occasion a brook trout pushes into the main stem from a tributary, but rainbow trout and whitefish only enter the water-shed below Deer Lodge, leaving the upper flowage a sanctuary for the hardy immigrant browns.

Stan Bradshaw and I trudged across the chalk flats through a swirling blow of tumbleweeds and dust. "It was a hard winter."

I strung a rod with the incurable optimism of an angler who cherishes a river. "What do you mean? Was?"

Life Stages of the Mayfly

Egg: The female deposits fertilized eggs by dropping them in mass from the air to the water, dapping them through contact of the abdomen on the water, or extruding them after submersion into the water. The eggs adhere to bottom rubble until the moment of hatching.

Nymph: The period of the aquatic stage of the cycle varies in different species from months to years. Nymphs cling to rocks, crawl over detritus, burrow in silt, or swim free. At emergence, the insects crawl out on stones or swim to the surface.

Dun (sub-imago): The dun is a stage of brief duration. The insect flies from the water to nearby trees or brush. On a perch of foliage, the opaque sheath splits as the dun molts to an adult spinner.

Spinner (imago): In their bright and agile stage, spinners gather in mating flights, and females deposit the eggs. The spinners then die and fall to land or water.

High profile imitation

Photo by Stan Bradshaw

Mist on the flat, slow water of the Upper Snake

Deep pupa

Emergent pupa

Trout swirling

Against outsweep bends of the stream, I plopped a weighted Muddler Minnow. With mended drifts I teased the fly across bands of deep current, slowly wading down the river towards a notch in the bank.

In spite of a sudden spatter of chilling rain, the trout at the bank's sheltered indentation rose with steady sipping motions. The fish were picking off fool-hardy emerging duns of the Blue-Winged Olive *(Baetis)* clinging to the surface in long floats.

I retreated, leaving the site unbothered, and searched upstream for Stan. "Do you want to see some rising trout?"

"You're kidding?"

Even the ever-present mud swallows abandoned the prowl of the air. The birds hid in sheltering burrows in the face of a cliff. Except for a scattering of mayfly duns and the presence of obliging trout, the river slid by in a barrenness of grey misery.

To study the feeding rhythm of the three working trout, we approached from the far side. "Not big."

Stan peered with the grim-faced concentration that masked his features whenever he stalked a position. "They're taking dry flies."

After fining down the leader tippet to attach a matching No. 20 Adams, we alternated casts with the rod. We puttered for the lowest trout in the line with the hope of turning all the fish in an unflustered sequence, and we carefully avoided too high a float line.

I reached a trout with a drift that skipped past a protruding willow branch. When the fly disappeared, I lifted the rod tip softly. I fussed, as I felt the hook scrape free of the jaw bone, "Damn barb missed."

Stan seldom grinned or laughed as he cast to a fish, exuding a nervous energy during a play of serious endeavor. He functioned with an intensity that blocked out anything other than the matter of chosen trout. Nothing seemed humorous until the post-mortem of an angling day.

He marked the second fish in the file with a series of precise slack-line drifts. He completely covered the rise position with drag-

117

less floats down the lane. "Fussy trout?"

"Aren't they always?"

On the fourth pass, the fish sipped the fly with a serene tip of the snout. The hooked trout plunged upstream past the lead riser to struggle for brush at the banks, but it skirted the root snarls without snagging the fine tippet.

Stan pressured the fish into the middle currents of the river, allowing thrashing and bulling until the battler wallowed feebly in near shallows. He then skidded the 14-inch brown trout onto the sand.

The fish displayed a fine condition for so soon after the tail of winter; both the trout and the mayflies were evidence of the momentary health of the river — the brown resplendent with a plump roundness to the body. In the wash of edge current it revived quickly to spurt into deeper water.

This set of opportunistic trout rose to mayflies, with no heed of an accompanying north wind. In a link of biological rhythm, as if mayfly and trout were responding inevitably to the same call, the presence of the insects gathered feeding fish to suitable water. The dun of the Blue-Winged Olive regulated the activity of the fish on that foul-weather day.

The delicate gentility of the mayfly epitomizes the fly fishing quest. During emergence most species of the order, unlike the caddis fly, ride the water in serene martyrdom to dry fresh wings, conditioning fish to a steady rise.

A no-drag dry fly presentation imitates this float of the dun. The pattern drifts, apparently unattached to the leader tippet, and the pull of varying currents straightens the fine, limp nylon without jerking the fly.

An artificial nymph that matches the pre-hatching mayfly also performs better with a natural presentation. In minor deviations of surface flow, the pattern wobbling with the drift imitates an insect pinned in the meniscus. The unweighted nymph with a greased

118

leader merits the same precise offering to individual trout as does the dry fly.

Too many fly fishermen fail to profit from pre-emergence characteristics of the mayfly. For hours before the actual migration to the surface, the nymphs rise and fall through the upper bands of current. In a restless period, immature insects drift downstream in trial hops.

With the flux of insect emergence, trout initially continue to feed on the nymphal stage. Plucking struggling insects in the surface film, fish roll with humping rises. But the feeders choose with extreme selectivity, not only on the basis of pattern features but also on minute differences in the depth of the fly, as they ignore the duns to pick the nymphs.

At luncheon prior to a guest-privilege day of fishing the pampered Shepaug River of Connecticut, we trailed to the backyard as Chester Tuttle demanded, "I want to see this wonder-child fly caster."

Beaming John Koenig handed his eleven year old daughter a 7½ foot glass rod, remarking in complete understatement, "She's pretty fair."

Jennifer slammed flawless loops of a double haul cast so fluidly that the follow appeared effortless until both tip-toed feet popped into the air. She placed 50 feet of line in an accurate fan at the edge of a wrought-iron fence. With curves, air rolls, and slack presentations, she performed all the required maneuvers of streamside strategy.

"There's a whole generation growing up like this," Chester marveled. "More so than ever."

"Heaven help the fish," I laughed softly.

In the afternoon, the bright sunlight subsided in the stream valley. The vigorous flow bounced on a gravel bed within the borders of a stately hardwood forest of elms and sycamores. The river jumbled in riffles over the rocky soil bed.

As we strung the rods, I asked Jenny, "Are there any special flies for this water?"

She pulled free a nymph from the wool patch of her vest, "There'll be a hatch of *Stenonema fuscum*."

Chester threw up his hands in protest, "Steno' who? What kind of talk is that from a little kid?"

I passed an emergent nymph with a frayed nylon-roll wing case, an innovation suggested by Ted Rogowski in "Crackerbarrel Discourses," and knotted one of the patterns onto my own leader. "Better try that, Chester," I grinned, "if your Royal Coachman doesn't work."

The coming mayfly emergence predicted an afternoon feeding on the nymph of the insect. In the hours prior to any sign of surface action, trout fell to a precise imitation. The nymph pattern fit the moment with all the conclusiveness of an ambush.

Chester and John, bankers from New York, fished the water below a stone bridge. Each staked a side of the stream with an upward approach. Neither fishermen displayed any rustiness from confinement within a big city work-week, plucking familiar pockets on this home stretch of river in deft strings of 10 to 13-inch trout.

Chester insisted later, when we crossed on a riffle, "I don't even own a Royal Coachman anymore."

Even with a burst of duns in the evening, when enough fish graduated to a top-water preference, I pitched the nymph to trout that continued to feed sub-surface and fooled a few of the best feeders that were snubbing dry fly passes.

Jenny pointed out the holding niche of a sizable trout, warning me about a curl of flow that billowed over a rock and would lift a sunken fly away from the fish unless the line rested on the inside band of water.

With bulging breaks, the gulper accepted four nymphs from the drift to every dun. It fed with a spurt rhythm, snatching four or five insects between 30-second rest periods, but it never culled a surface-riding adult except on the initial pop of a string of rises.

120

I nabbed the fish with a nymph, but I played the 16-inch brown carelessly and lost it when the hook ripped free of the tongue. I watched the fading of a butter-yellow flank. "That's a long-line release," I said to John.

John glimpsed his daughter at the bend. "I'd appreciate it if you could giver her some hints."

The child crouched at the tail of a curving run. She lifted the line to place a fly on the water, mending to delay any drag and keeping the nymph drifting with the current. On the following cast to a rising trout, she set the hook with the nonchalant ease of expectation.

"Just put her on different types of rivers now," I offered. "Expose her to a range of experience."

She understood the cycle of the insects of the stream. She cast a fly with a finely attuned sense of the imitative to the rhythm of the water. With an entomological foundation, she already possessed the key to the behavior of trout.

For the mayfly dun, the critical factor of imitation with hackleless patterns, either the Swisher/Richards No-Hackle or the Caucci/Nastasi Compara-Dun*, is the height of the artificial wing. As with the natural insect, this upright feature is the initial characteristic of an object entering the "window" of trout vision. A realistic length of wing material is an important point of selectivity.

But the spinner of the mayfly, dying after mating, falls to the water with wings neither up nor down. The death spasm lingers for crucial moments, wings sagging slowly from a middle cant. The mayfly often topples to one side, to drift with only a single wing flush on the surface.

A spinner fall achieves an important role in trout feeding. All the females of a species that have emerged in a sporadic tempo of

---

*The Compara-Dun of Al Caucci and Bob Nastasi was a separate development based on the venerable precedent of the no-hackle Haystack, a durable fly pattern long used on the West Branch of the Ausable.

121

hours suddenly die in mass over the water, the insects scattering randomly on the surface and sparking a general rise.

Even the miniscule spinner of the *Tricorythodes*, matched with a No. 28 hook, excites trout. On placid currents of a river, a plethora of prone bodies offers an easily attainable meal. The mayfly rigidly patterns fish into the gentlest of sipping motions.

The absolute avoidance of drag, more so than with an imitation of the dun, proves crucial in the simulation of a spinner. Often a direct downstream slack-cast presents the fly in the most unhindered fashion. The pattern, drifting straight ahead of the leader, escapes any minor cross-squibble of current.

Simon "Cougar" Randolph contacted me in September, "Why don't you come on over and help me figure out these tiny black mayflies?"

Cougar earned that prideful nickname — after his father had already appropriated the tag of "Bear" — due to his height and heft of size. The entire male segment of this pioneer family grew to a 300 pound brawn that doubled the ordinary proportions of a man.

All week we tied matching imitations of the *Tricorythodes* spinner during a heavy fall on the Big Hole River. Late each night we arranged completed patterns of numerous versions, rushing out each morning to display the flies to the scrutiny of fish.

Coug waded into position at a big flat of water. With determined patience, he withheld his casts from the unpocked flow. He stood above a slot of deep and smooth current, awaiting the activity that promised to bloom furiously over this stretch.

The flight of mayflies bunched in a communal dance. Rising and falling in the air, the sparkling hoard dropped ever nearer the river. The females, in resolute abandonment, sifted from the hovering group to splash to the surface in a watery finish.

Coug spotted the sips of initial rises. "They were just sitting there waiting."

The water already appeared gritty with a pepper sprinkle of black bodies. "It's going to be a real dumper."

122

I slouched there on the bank for nearly half an hour, watching Coug cast skillfully to the trout. I missed nothing: a pattern of failure repeated itself, as the fish disdained imitative flies during the opening minutes of spinner abundance.

Then in the last hour and a half of this two-hour fall, poly-wing patterns, a prototype by Barry Beck, started to account for nice trout. The no-hackle fly with flush wings of polypropolene yarn suddenly gained complete acceptability to the fussy trout.

We hunched over the vises that night to create more of the minute imitations, even deviating from the no-hackle concept to construct tiny buzz patterns. "The problem has to be with these wings."

Coug offered the sharp ideas of an observant angler, but possessing only a spotty acquaintance with fly fishing history he tended to hail any thought as a stroke of innovation. "For clear wings? Why don't we leave them off entirely? They're invisible."

"That's been noted."

"So? Why use them?"

"The flush wings still leave an imprint. The trout rise mainly to a spinner's indentation pattern."

In the morning, I reassumed a vigil at the edge of the stream for a third day of observation: 1st day — trout; 2nd day — angler; 3rd day — insect. I wondered about the habits of the spinner that might affect the first quarter of feeding time, and not affect the rest of the activity.

When I watched the first fresh spinners drop to the water, I noticed the raised angle of the wings. I splashed into the line of drift to observe more closely that the wings of all the insects stood free of the surface film. "Cut off the wings," I called to Coug.

"I thought you said that wouldn't work?"

"Just try it."

After performing the streamside surgery, he presented the altered pattern to a rising trout. He slid faultless drifts to cover the snouts of feeders. "No good."

123

Fly tied by Barry Beck.   Photo by Glen Zander.

No Hackle Spinner
of the Tricorythodes

I pulled a full hackle fly from the box. With careful snips I trimmed all the rooster fibers except the outlines of two up-canted wings. "Try this one."

Coug offered the fly* to the same snobbish fish, putting the float perfectly over trout sidling in efficient gathering. He lifted the rod a bit too hard as the pattern disappeared. "It worked," he grumped, holding the sheared tippet.

"I don't believe it."

When spinners drifted long enough to filter from the upper currents, with their wings becoming sodden on the water, poly-wing patterns once more effectively fooled the trout. The intermix of droop-wing and up-wing mayflies progressively shifted in percentage, until at the cessation of the fall only older, bedraggled insects lingered on the surface.

After the glut by the trout on spinners, we still watched the river. "You don't think," Coug asked, "that the clipped wings made a difference?"

"It's hard to believe the difference between translucent wings in the air and no wings in the air is all that significant."

He offered a basic truism of fly fishing, "We'll let the trout judge."

For the early moments of a rise, we fished for five days in alternating periods of equal time with no-wing and fiber-wing versions. We tallied 32 trout on the winged fly and 14 trout on the unwinged fly, with a similarly disproportionate spread for the duration of the testing.

"Maybe it's the way the sunlight strikes the wings," I conceded.

The simple expediency of changing patterns, up-wing early and droop-wing late, added 4 or 5 trout to the total each morning. For

---

*In *A Modern Dry Fly Code*, Vincent Marinaro suggests this method of representing wings for the no-hackle Sulphur Spinner.

gimlet-eyed fish in gentle water of the flats, a single feature on a No. 28 hook seemed to determine the accomplishment of the fakery.*

Perhaps the fascination of angling never falters because a fisherman never masters more than the generalities of catching trout. It is a game of specific moments and unique problems. Fish vary so much in habit and feeding routine from stream to stream that it is impossible to make dogmatic rules.

But it is also impossible to attack each fish as a unique and limitless challenge. Even without definite rules, an angler eliminates most plans of approach. From study and experience, a fly fisherman narrows the possibilities with his guesses at the specific "problem" offered by each fish.

A basic understanding of the life-cycle of aquatic insects aids a fly fisherman in two ways: it gives him both a knowledge of moments of peak vulnerability, when an insect species is most exposed to fish predation, and an understanding of distinctive motion, where the insect species is selectively identified to the fish predation.

A studious fly fisherman learns the major mayflies along a favorite trout stream. During a season of note-taking, specimens are gathered and dates recorded. This information correlates into an invaluable emergence table for a specific area.

These stream notes develop into a calendar of prediction for a season of average rainfall and temperature. As the same mayfly species emerge yearly within the same span of dates, the angler grows attuned to the pulse of the water, waiting in readiness for the successive appearances of the insects.

---

*General tackle fails to suffice; a specifically integrated outfit is more crucial to success in the "micro situation" than in any other aspect of fly fishing:

Rod: over 7½ ft., with a delicate tip to cushion the strike and protect the leader tippet.

Line: a #3 or #4 line for minimal water-drag during the setting of the hook.

Leader: a 6X to 8X tippet section of no less than 26 inches, the 40% terminus of the leader made of soft nylon and the 60% butt tied with stiff nylon.

Hook: a fine wire, up-eye hook (always knotted with a Double Turle).

Chapter 11

The Salmon Fly —
Willow Fly Excitement

F ROM ITS HEAD-WATERS on Sapphire Mountain, the stream tumbles within a ruggedness of natural pomp. The course threads through forests of lofty pine on the middle stretches. In the lower reaches, Rock Creek jams through granite canyons, leaving trees on the cliffs stunted with the scant growing room.

The small river twists in a procession of pockets and rapids. For over fifty miles it carries pure trout water, which harbors profuse insect populations of stone flies, mayflies, and caddis flies. With its pollution-intolerant Salmon Fly *(Pteronarcys californica),* the water shed boasts the highest abundance of this giant stone fly on the western slope of the Continental Divide.

Rock Creek rates as one of the blue ribbon trout waters of Montana; but this is a dubious honor in a state that touts the stream in order to attract fishermen and then perversely refuses to protect the quality of the fishery. In accessible lower stretches near the highway, the river badly requires no-kill regulations.

A crotchety bait fisherman stumped along the bank one day, "Blue ribbon trout stream, my eye. Damn near fished out is what it is. More of these worthless whitefish here now than anything else."

"Did you do any good at all?" I persisted.

"No, just a few 10 inchers," he opened his creel to display four rainbows, "and lots of whitefish."

"Where are the whitefish?"

"I tossed them back," he complained. "No, to catch any decent trout you have to go twenty miles up. Too many damn whitefish down here."

"Some wonder," I grunted.

Rock Creek suffers from environmental dangers — clear-cut lumbering on the tributaries, subdivision developments on the flood plain, excessive trout-kill on lower portions — to which state and federal regulatory agencies react only under extreme public pressure.

Fortunately the Missoula region contains an environmentally aware cadre, which musters the needed sentiment to affect decisions. Through efforts of conservation groups, adverse policies have currently been stopped or mitigated in the worst instances.

The population of the *Pteronarcys* stone fly even became an issue in the proposal hearings for running a paved road, a Forest Service boondoggle, besides the entire length of the creek. The ensity of the salmon fly female to lay eggs on a black surface during any rainstorm pointed out one of the undesirable effects of replacing dirt ruts with a macadam thoroughfare.

During an evening of June, our car jounced along the dirt set of wheel tracks, a blessed deterrence for easy-time visitors to the creek. The shock springs of the vehicle squawked with every bump along the 25-mile drive to Cougar Campground.

In the waning light, we hastily pitched a sagging tent and heated cans of stew over a small fire. "Tomorrow morning," I said as we unrolled the sleeping bags, "don't wake me up — not for the glory of any frigid dawn."

128

Joe Marsana spread the foot of his extra-long mummy roll clear out the flaps. "When do we start?"

"If you want to fish, go ahead and use nymphs right here. But later on, for the adult flights, we'll run about 7 miles downstream."

When I ventured free of the tent in the lingering morning chill, I appreciated the pot of cocoa ready on the grill. I restoked the dead fire to warm the drink. I grabbed a cup of hot brew and retreated to the shelter of the sleeping bag.

At noon, when I found my lanky partner engaged in his gallop of high-stepping haste, he stopped rambling along the stream, "You lazy son-of-a-buck."

"How long have you been out here?"

"Since 4 a.m.," he chided. "and it's been fabulous."

In the fields, spring tufts of bear grass stood in bowed plumage. Buttercups and wild daisies crowded above a greenery of ground ferns. Saw-edged grass waved at waist-level in a mild breeze of the warming day.

At the next upstream run, I also discovered a concentration of trout. I hooked a hefty fish, the rash of action enough to momentarily spoil an angler; and I uncautiously pressured the 19-inch rainbow into a performance of aerial contortions.

Joe dallied on the bank to watch the finish. "I've never seen fish fight like these."

I slid the trout free into the water. "They're wild fish, not super-market rainbows dumped in; but sometimes I think they take the term 'wild' too seriously."

"Amen," he grinned.

We tromped a famed stretch of Rock Creek, the Hog Back and Double Hog Back, through the remainder of the afternoon. Leap-frogging as we shared prime areas, we often huddled to offer bits of advice. In answer to shouts, we aided each other in landing especially notable trout.

While Joe probed the edge of a white-water rapids, I sat on the

130

rocks. "You're not going to get a fish yet."

"Why not?"

"Keep moving down."

Discarded nymphal husks sticking to stones acted as a sign-post for a migration route. Where the current tumbled too fast at the head of the rip, no empty shells littered the beach. And at the slow pan of flow near the tail of the run, no skins crusted the rocks.

Joe approached the moderate center-region with a drop-down series of retrieves. He allowed the fly to swing on a short line until it almost reached across the stream, teasing the stone fly pattern out of the middle into quieter water at the river edge.

The line jumped with a bolting strike. "This is a trophy," Joe hollered.

The silver fighter tore across the currents so fast, bouncing over the turbid flow, that the reel buzzed in a mad clicking until the spool overspun. The fish thumped a single time against the taut line while Joe futilely scrambled on the bank.

My partner wandered back down. "You're right," he conceded, "they're not hatchery rainbows."

"We'll miss the dry fly action if we stay here," I warned.

He covered the migration-lanes with a series of fanning casts. "Who cares?"

Trucks and cars raced along the road in trailing dust swirls, an assemblage of fishermen from a scattering of states, all on hand for the madness of the salmon fly, all in the search of that "hot" portion of the stream

With a 3-year residence in the river, the giant stone fly leads an incomplete life-cycle* (egg/nymph/adult) that culminates in an early summer emergence. The hatch of all mature nymphs occurs on a stretch of water within a matter of days. The insects respond in

---

*A "complete" entomological life-cycle includes a pupal stage.

mass with a survival design of so glutting fish and birds that the sheer numbers ensure a successful mating process.

At peak flights of the adult salmon fly, a river surface flows strangely devoid of feeding trout. Only random pops interrupt the clumsy wallow of insects in the current. After the rush of an opening frenzy, fish retire through the height of the activity for necessary digestion.

Prime moments of opportunity for a fly fisherman coincide with the gorging mayhem of the trout, twin periods arriving at the beginning of both the nymph migration and the adult fall; and the "head" of the flurries progresses upriver a few miles each day.

Any fine imitation of the *Pteronarcys* nymph — Grove Hull's Stonefly, Cal Bird's Salmon Fly, Ed Mueller's Brown Fork Tail, Charles Brooks' Montana Stone — prove effective in mimicking the migration crawl. With a steady hand-twist retrieve, these weighted flies bob over the rocks in the manner of the natural. At the proper moment, matching nymphs produce trout.

But it is the frenzy of adult insects — not any magnificent angling with a sunken technique — that triggers the famed news that spreads across the land. The appearance of the salmon fly on the stream launches the message to fly fishermen.

Anglers check the emergence progress with telephone calls to tackle shops along the rivers, "How far up?"

The hatch advances up a water-shed. Clambering adults — with salmon-orange bellies that lend the name — cluster at streamside in every tree and shrub for miles along the banks. Lumbering 2-inch insects gather on the brush in this surplus after their escape from the water.

When the heat of day warms the wing muscles of the salmon fly, careening flights occur over the water. Near noon-hour, the clumsy adults tilt into a laboring bustle of motion; and as if suddenly stripped of power, the flyers glide onto the surface with splashes of calamity.

With the beginning of the insect fall, the carnival of the giant

132

stone fly — with the attendant spectacle of huge fish erupting through the water — bursts into dominant activity. The adults splat in a living deluge, keying the trout population of a river into a mass excess of feeding.

On one unique stretch of water, natural scenery plays an almost equal part with the moment of the salmon fly: in the tortured rapids of Bear Trap Canyon of the Madison, the river poses a close rivalry to the salmon fly excitement.

Doug Wynter strained on the oars to hold the rubber raft on the lip of a white churn. He slid the boat into the chute, releasing control to the currents, and he stroked with the bucking rolls of the slide. Each time the raft swung around, he yanked its nose to the front.

Lounging against the back tubing of the doughnut, Mel Sneedman rested a single hand on the grip-rope. He sat in roly-poly nonchalance in an orange life-jacket, while the spray doused his pipe. He gazed at passing walls of rock or at looming humps of boulder.

As we poked deeper through intermittent maelstroms of water, we gained the difficult access to the canyon; and there, on the clinging scrub vegetation, we spotted vanguard specimens of the insect emergence and searched quiet eddies of the river for signs of rising trout.

After slipping through one of these tumbles of water-fury, Doug unexpectedly beached the raft. "The rower needs a break," he conceded.

The pool proved to be a focal area of the stonefly fall. As the morning light slanted into the canyon, the water popped with initial explosions. At the edges of the bowl, the flow collected enough adult flyers to attract trout.

Doug lost a thrashing rainbow of 5 pounds, cursing the fish with poetic blasphemy. He slapped casts over each subsequent disturbance, chasing boils of feeding trout with a hasty jog up and down the shore.

133

I also indulged in this random flogging of rise-circles. And I knew, as he knew, the folly of pursuing spots that only marked a formerly present fish. But in that visible crowd of elusive behemoth trout, I forgot any semblance of patience.

Only Mel covered the water in a reasoned pattern. With an induced splat of the adult version of Bird's Salmon Fly, he hit a single patch of holding current in repetitive persistence, calmly working the area until a searching fish discovered the surface disturbance.

"First trout," Mel announced, passing down the shoreline.

At that moment, by a fluke, one of my sloppy casts also hooked a frisky 3 pound fish. "A fly isn't safe out there," we laughed.

We trailed towards the next spill of rapids. Shy of the fast water, we forced the trout into quiet shallows and landed the fish. After admiring the wild colors of each rainbow-sided beauty and gloating momentarily over our good fortune at being there in the Bear Trap, we returned the natural-stock to the river.

At that moment, an enormous form shattered the flow of an eddy. The fish vanished in a wash of ripples, while I pointed to the precise mark. "Go ahead," I offered.

"Too big for me," Mel grinned. "I'd better not even try for that one."

At the specific portion of the drift, I grouped a sequence of casts, waiting for that particular trout to circle again in a cruising path. I ignored the surrounding commotion of feeding fish and slapped eight or nine floats over the niche.

The same trout crashed the muddy water to arc above the No. 2 fly. It fell upon the spot and obliterated any sight of the pattern, but the fish had snatched the hook. It tore downstream towards the squeeze of canyon.

I chased on jumbled boulders of the beach. As Mel followed the race — shouting impossible advice, "You have to stop him!" — I pressed down the narrowing strip. I edged next to an impassable wall above the swath of hissing current. After tottering there on the

134

pin of the ledge too long, I wrapped a grip on the peeling backing to save my line and stuck the rod straight at the rip to break off the headlong trout.

Mel slumped down to a seat on a flat stone, his face pale under forelocks of white hair, and he puffed deep breaths of air. For the first time that day, he removed the pipe from his lips. "I can't run like that," he wheezed.

Doug sprinted down the beach to his father-in-law. "Are you all right?"

"I'm fine now," Mel insisted.

I squatted beside the man. "Is there anything we can do?"

The ruddiness of color slipped back into his cheeks, and his chest settled to an even rise and fall. "I have to take it easier now, because I had a mild heart attack 3 years ago."

"I don't know if this is any place to take it easy."

He stood to gaze at the plummet of descent down the river. "That was some fish."

"Wasn't it?"

"When I get too excited, you know" — he picked up his rod — "I just start thinking about a barren piece of Eastern water in August."

"Does it work?"

"If it did," he smiled mischievously as he resumed the walk upstream, "I wouldn't come here every year."

For the fly fisherman who has not been jaded by the mad splendor of the Giant Stonefly emergence, the rivers provide an only slightly less thumping diminuendo. The inch-long adult Willow Fly excites trout to the same surface-blasting rises as the salmon fly.

In many watersheds, these insects intermix at the highest elevation of the *Pteronarcys* and at the lowest of the *Acroneuria*. The mating flights of the two genera combine to compound the frenzy. But Willow Fly hatches exist also as singularly important events occuring throughout the summer on major Rocky Mountain rivers.

135

I regaled Harold Habein with the glory of fuzzy angling over wary trout, ending with a qualification for the primitive-area Big Salmon River. "But we probably won't have to worry about matching the hatch here."

"That won't bother the boys."

In the morning, we studied the process of emergence as the willow fly nymphs crawled from the water to the top of a rock to split the skin along the back. We protected some still wet bodies of golden adults from a hoard of foraging birds.

Above us, an eagle glided with the valley thermals, as our group hiked the short spur trail up the river. The boys sprinted ahead in a flush of exuberant energy, spooking mule deer and ground squirrels off the path.

I picked predominant duns off the streamside foliage and showed the insects to Doctor Habein. "But the fly won't make a big difference to the fish."

"What would you use?" the doctor asked.

I searched through my boxes of patterns, taking out a No. 14 Beaverkill Red Fox and holding it up against the blue-grey living insect. "This one is close."

When we reached the river-head at the outlet of a lake, I prepared to fish. Since the Red Fox nestled in my hand, I knotted it onto the tippet and then watched the jaunty little Fox ride among the rocks and washes to swirl with the pocket water.

The hatch of mayflies grew heavier as the morning warmed, rushes of duns popping from bounces of the river. The first six floats with a Red Fox caught cutthroat trout. "Any fly would work now," I added.

Abundant wild fish rose to the Red Fox at every crease and pot-hole. Each bright fish dashed recklessly and splashed clumsily when it felt the pull of hook. The released trout blended into the clear water to fade over the paleness of the gravel.

The mayfly emergence continued undiminished, but at noon the first lumbering yellow stone flies flew a preparatory path over

136

the water. The insects circled high and dove low to skitter onto the river. They floundered for only a moment before disappearing with the chug of a trout.

The specimen I cupped in my hands was the common Western species, known to anglers as the willow fly or the water cricket, but the insect was larger in size and lighter in color than samples of the same species collected from lower altitude rivers earlier in the year. The straw yellow stonefly was imitated by a No. 6 pattern; whereas the upper Bitterroot River specimens were light brown and the size of a No. 8 match.

I resumed angling, with the Red Fox still on the tippet since the mayfly hatch remained heavy. I focused attention not so much on my casting as on an increasing number of willow flies in the air and on the water, and on the feeding frenzy of trout leaping and slashing for the insects. Without noticing a slack-off in the rate I hooked fish, I continued to cast until the little Red Fox was not catching any trout at all.

In the rough riffle water of a wilderness river teeming with avidly feeding trout, a fly matching the numerically dominant insect on the water failed to fool the fish. The wild cutthroat displayed a modicum of selectivity.

I waded up to the river head to meet Dr. Habein and young Jared beside the stream. They were also watching the growing orgy caused by suicide crashes of the stone flies. Jared pointed out a scoop of deeper, quieter water against the far bank, "We saw a nice fish jump over there."

We watched the half-moon patch of water and calculated that two trout were feeding, one high and one low on the line of drift, each cruising for stone flies that curled into the area from the current. Dr. Habein suggested, "Try them."

"I bet they won't take the Red Fox."

My cast snubbed hard above and beyond the distant shore to pull coils of slack line onto the faster intervening current. The fly lazed prettily on the slow pace of the pocket. Drifts with the Fox

137

paraded unsuccessfully as trout pursued the erratic stone flies.

I picked out a No. 6 Soft Pillow, which was darker than the natural willow fly, but the hair-wing of the pattern lay flat along the back to outline the proper silhouette. Apparently the shape and size of the fly passed as critical factors of selectivity.

Twice the Sofa Pillow landed well enough, gliding freely among the trout but the splashing, flailing struggle of live insects attracted the striking flurry. The third cast landed alone in a gaggle of falling stone flies, and the cutthroat at the bottom end of the flow gobbled the fake.

I bulled the fish into a current of fast water to leave the second feeding trout undisturbed. As it swung downstream, I forced the rambunctious cutthroat across to a quiet flow at the near edge. I tired and landed the 15½-inch fish.

I handed the rod to 14-year-old Jared, explaining the mechanics of the "check" cast. "Now pop it higher."

He waded deeper into the riffle, a boy who had never used a fly rod before the trip began but who now was a veteran of over seventy trout, and put the fly across. On the fifth float into the hollow, he hooked the second cutthroat and played out the fish. With a prac- ticed hand, he released the twin of the first trout.

We started back to camp for a hot supper. We followed the path among mountain ferns, tarrying to pick huckleberries from the hillside, musing upon the vagaries of trout in general. I explained to Harold and Jared that these cutthroat were not supposed to feed selectively. "The only ones who are never really wrong about what they want are the trout themselves."

We threaded along the trail away from the river to leave the trout and stone flies to their necessary ritual — a bond of survival by which the required insanity of the one was structured by the basic instinctual design of the other.

138

Chapter 12

The Grasshopper Frenzy

As THE RAFT DRIFTED in a lazy float around a corner of the Clark Fork River, puffs of a land breeze carried the fragrance of fresh-mown grass. The sputter of a reaper beat with syncopated rhythm through the slap of the cutting wheel. The machine was mowing a swath through a field of high grass in a line tracing a curl of the river.

Flustered hoards of grasshoppers flew in front of the reaper blade in high loops that carried a cloud of insects over the steep bank. The rain of hoppers splatted onto a slope of deep water. Trout boiled along the sweeping path of the falling fare, tearing the slick of river to a froth.

John Chist muttered with a mild oath, "What the..."

"Get a fly in there," I ordered.

The drifting boat passed the bend even with the reaper. A long cast smacked a hopper imitation into the churning trout, and a fish jumped the fly on the first twitch. The struggle lasted only a moment as the heavy trout pulled towards deep water and tore free of the hook-hold.

At the rear of the boat, John played a splashing rainbow of 3 pounds. "Reminds me of bass belting a school of shad."

Against a grass clump trailing in the water, a bulging, mottled back split the surface, a trout snatching the Letort Hopper with the turn and chugging into the shallows among rooted weeds to bang its jaw in an attempt to dislodge the nuisance grasp of the hook.

Glen Simmons rowed from the middle seat of the john-boat. He chided, "How are you fighting that hog?" But he nodded when I pumped, "Take it to him."

The sunlight of late afternoon slanted with sharp rays that blurred color to a shimmering pastel wash. Objects faded in indistinct silhouettes against the reflected haze. A fly on the sparkle of water drifted lost to a fisherman, causing a rash of missed strikes.

When the worker in the hayfield shifted the reaper into neutral gear, the thump of the engine still beat the air. But as the machine ceased to move, grasshoppers no longer fell to the river, and the trout vanished to deeper water.

The only remaining hooked fish bucked against a straining rod hoop. It surged with sudden dashes, with each run peeling line from the crotchety reel disc; but as the trout rested between the sprints, lifts tipped the grudging brute in reluctant skids towards the surface.

"Hopper madness!" We scooped my 6½-pound brown, garbed in a salad of bottom weeds. "It makes them foolish."

When the farmer had cleared the blade of his machine, the cutting wheel kicked into gear in a gasp of hitches. The forward lurch signaled a resumption of the glory-fall of grasshoppers, while I climbed to exchange seats with Glen; after a pause, the trout again ripped the gentle flow at the bend.

I stroked carefully to muffle any noise from the oarlocks, while I kept the casters within range of fish, but my rowing inexperience only sidled the front end of the boat toward shore. "That's all right,"

John encouraged. "Let Glen get one of them."

Grasshoppers flopped onto the river in the curved shape of a scimitar blade, outwards to a distance of 3 or 4 feet. Within that arc, fish jammed in a packed milling that paced evenly downstream with the fall. The biggest trout cruised nearest to the grass sweepers.

Glen panicked in a moment of buck-fever, when he tangled his cast by snagging the fly in the unfolding line; neither John nor I helped with our exclamations, "There's one that'll go 10 pounds!"

The pattern bounced off the bank slightly ahead of the unnatural "hatch." As the fly hopped to the water, the river-patch exploded with a tangle of fish. A huge brown trout ruptured the spot, only to lose in the flurry, as another jumper pirated the hook.

The hulk of the rust-pitted reaper, an unlikely gift from paradise, turned the corner away from the river. Confusion on the water ceased in a sudden calm. Only fishermen playing trout lingered as a reminder of the unbelievable 7 or 8 minutes that had yielded three fish of over 2 pounds.

Glen released an 18-inch rainbow, shrugging resignedly as this final trout bolted into dark water. "Wonder if the guy will sell that machine to us?"

"My hands are still shaky," John laughed softly.

They were visitors to a fabled land of trout, who had never seen anything like this anywhere else; but it was my home, and I had never before witnessed anything like that either — never such a tumultuous exhibit of the many large trout these rivers hide in deeper holds.

"Hey," I grumbled in mock complaint, when we drifted without casting past the overhung debris of a fallen tree, "are you going to fish, or are you going to sit there and reminisce?"

The grasshopper imitation is not strictly a pattern for big fish or large rivers. Often tiny flows meander through prime land of open meadows, and in these narrow streams, grass hangs over the

banks on each side to lure many hoppers to the water.

My 3-year-old daughter Heather fishes on spring-run Willow Creek. She creeps with due caution to the edge to dap a fly on the surface. As she flails and slaps a Joe's Hopper on the water, 6 to 10-inch brookies rush from undercut banks to latch onto the fly.

Any fish foolish enough to hook itself is promptly hauled kicking up the weed bunkers into the grass. "Get him, daddy."

I unhook the fish. "Do you want to let him go home to his mother?"

"His mommy...crying."

"Definitely," I agree, and she dismisses each trout with a jaunty wave and proceeds to stalk the next likely patch of open stream.

Already she is particular about the character of water she is prospecting. If the stream-bed is too shallow, she passes the spot when she sees no fish. She seeks the dark little slots of undercut current that scoop out depressions in the soft dirt.

The same pothole-shooting techniques are essential on broad expanses of large streams. On small jump-across creeks, stranded grasshoppers soon disperse on diverging currents to all channels of the flow, but on rivers, the insects quickly sink in the rougher water before spreading towards the center.

In the shallows, a trout holds snug in dish-size hollows of the bottom. The head of the fish points into currents that ebb from the main flow. A trout angles slightly towards the middle of the stream, swirling about to snatch terrestrials that drop to the water:

Dick Fryhover, one of the best hopper fishermen on Western rivers, uses a greased Muddler to bust out 35 to 40 mid-summer brown trout over 4 pounds. "Twelve inches from the bank is too far," he insists. "The fly should land within 6 inches so that it doesn't hit the fish on the head."

In close, simple dapping performs well even for a sophisticated fisherman. The angler treads lightly on the bank to minimize telltale vibrations. He kneels back from the water, poking the rod tip beyond the edge to plop the fly on the surface.

For months, I tossed a grasshopper pattern against willow tangles below the railroad trestle on the Clark Fork in Deer Lodge. The pattern bobbing at the edge of the sticks caught nice trout up to 3 pounds, but within the maze of brambles, there are promising scoops of clear water that the best of drifts never reach.

I crossed over down-river and entered the thicket. I squirmed through tight clumps of tree stems, crawling through the last barrier of dead-fall limbs to sprawl onto a circle of dirt next to the water.

While I rested the spot from my entry commotion, doubting if my arrival warranted the effort, I studied the pit of dark river swirling under the branches. I sprung a fly out with a bow and arrow cast onto the slick-litter of foam and leaves.

The No. 6 Grasshopper curled in a slow dally on a slack leader, drifting to the edge of the submerged sticks. As it spread a wake with the twitch of a retrieve, it suddenly flushed down into the suck of an engulfing maw, the mouth resembling nothing so much as a scoop of a garbage barrel, and with a roll of the fish, the fly parted easily from the OX tippet.

Dapping is a way to reach specific niches against a bank. The particular drawback of the method is that each approach requires time. A common technique of casting grasshopper patterns on Western rivers is a more efficient manner of covering the water.

Rather than fishing towards the center on these broad tumbling trout streams, the angler wades out to the middle and casts back to the edge. This simple stratagem is precious on the riffle chop sections of rivers like the Madison, Jefferson, and Yellowstone, which are bordered by grasshopper meadows.

On a morning when an expected emergence of mayflies fizzled after the pop of a few sporadic specimens, this method of approach also proved a salvation on an Eastern flow: on the Delaware River, a hopper drift against the bank turned over lurking trout.

Cliff Schneider and Wynne Morris pointed out favored water along the stream. "It's tough fishing, though," Cliff warned, "when there's no hatch."

"Let's give it a chance."

During an hour of casting, the riffle breaks yielded only stray small rainbows. In the chop of pocket water, fish ignored offerings of dry flies and nymphs. Only a small Muddler Minnow, drifting over pot-holes in the center of the river, tapped 12 to 13-inch fish.

When I turned around to prospect the inside edge of current, I expected only more small trout in the shallow water. I flipped the Muddler in nonchalant drifts onto indented bowls of flow that spun against the rocks.

Cliff and Wynne stopped casting to proffer jibes. "The poor guy's confused."

"The river's this way."

But a grasshopper drift tallied bright silver rainbows of 16 and 17 inches within the next 10 minutes, super-charged trout that tore on long runs and bounced with high leaps, convincing my skeptical friends to fish water where they usually stood to cast.

Deep-water runs that curl into the soft earth of the bank pose a different problem. If the shadows of overhanging shrubs reach over the river, then trout remain near the lip of the slot, but if the sun angles down into the flow, the fish retreat into darkness.

In these currents at the outside bends of a meandering trout river, the nymph-like upstream presentation of a Joe's Hopper nabs deep-lying fish. A dead-drift fly sinks to a level visible to trout huddled into the undercut. The same fish that prove unsusceptible to surface patterns rush to the edge to snatch the wet Hopper.

Among a selection of grasshopper imitations, I carry two basic patterns: for sub-surface imitation, I wrap an underbody of copper wire on a Joe's Hopper; for a top-water fly, I tie a supply of the Letort Hopper. Also, ever-present in my fly books, I stock general simulations created with the Muddler Minnow and the Plain Jane Brown.

These grasshopper patterns extend the prime fishing of a mid-summer day. Once the sun warms up the fields, there are few better

145

imitations to cast on a meadow river. Until the evening chill — from 10:00 a.m. to 6:00 p.m. — these flies simulate a common food item of trout.

But fish grow selective with an abundance of the natural fare. On weeks of the "grasshopper wind," when warm breezes lift the clumsy insects over the water, trout develop a choosiness that demands a proper silhouette and size of imitation.

On many streams, a general representation — Rebel Joe, Cooper's Hopper, Neal's Hopper — fools grasshopper-crazed feeders. But on other flows, the fussy trout refuse all but the best pattern — and on these waters the Letort Hopper stands as the top choice.

In the sparkling *Crackerbarrel Discourses,* Ted Rogowski's collection of fly tying episodes, Ernest Schwiebert recounts the development of this pattern:

> The Letort Hopper is a synthesis of other hopper imitations. Letort fish were rejecting the traditional Michigan Hopper, Joe's Hopper and the Fore-and-Aft flies of Bergman — rising to inspect and refusing. Sometimes in the West, with less selective fish and bigger natural hoppers, I had used Muddler Minnows soaked in Silicone. Re-thinking the silhouette and light-pattern problems implicit in hoppers, I came up with these conclusions — that hackled flies floated too high and created a hackle collar light pattern that was poor and that real hoppers are linear in silhouette. I got several Letort fish to take weed stems when the hoppers were small and this caused some thinking. The first flies were tied to imitate these fledgling-size hoppers, and were quite simple — yellow nylon wool pulled apart and dubbed into the body, and a muddler-like system of deer hair. To permit the body to float flush in the surface, the deer hair is trimmed out under the throat. This system worked until the naturals were full grown, and then we found that returning to turkey wings like the traditional hoppers improved the silhouette again, the trailing deer hair suggesting both wing mass and kickers, as well as floating the fly.

146

This hopper, patterned for the discriminating fish of the Letort, seldom fails to interest even fussy trout. On flows from the Cowichan River of Vancouver to the Muscanetcong River of New Jersey, the fly succeeds where other surface imitations pass untouched over the most finicky beggars.

There are other states even more vociferous in an isolationist creed than Montana, but signs and bumper stickers also proliferate in picturesque regions of this one: "Don't Californicate Montana." It is a legitimate sentiment, not particularly directed at California the state, but at California as a symbol of the disfiguring greed of overdevelopment. There lingers a bitterness over those out-of-state people who come to Montana to buy and close the land as private preserves to escape the self-engendered stink of their home-ground.

Only a small portion of O'Dell Creek, near Ennis, remains open to access. With permission of the local owners, granted on polite request, a party of anglers is allowed to explore the rich spring-flow niches of a pasture stretch.

We ambled idly along a cow path, no longer fishing after the dwindling of morning mayflies; nevertheless, we studied the blank surface of the creek. As we disturbed grass fringes, we startled grasshoppers in every direction.

I trapped a hopper and tossed it onto an upstream riffle. As it spun along the drift, we ventured predictions on the moment of a rise. "Now," Ken Parkany said, but as the insect passed the upper lip of the pool he added, "Nothing is interested."

When the hopper hesitated on the slow pan of flow over the deepest water, I guessed, "Maybe now."

The surface broke with a golden swirl when a brown trout engulfed the hapless prey. "You take him," Steve Parkany insisted, as if my random prediction entitled me to the chance.

I sneaked behind the holding lair to present a sunken pattern. I curled an initial cast nicely down the center water, but when the line-tip pulled upsteream in a vigorous draw, I struck with inatten-

147

tive futility and tossed the fly back into a tree.

My partners crowed with belly-laughs from their position on the bank. "Now you know" — I picked the hook from the tangle of branches — "what not to do."

We captured more hoppers and threw them to drift in procession on the lane of current. We chummed for ten minutes, until the same trout rose, and continued to rise; Ken and I chased jumping hoards of insects, while Steve knotted a dry fly to his tippet.

He persisted until a timed drift matched the rise-rhythm of the feeder, but then on a lunging strike the trout missed the fly, or Steve missed the fish. He ripped the line off the water in a gurgling spray of drops, muttering softly to himself as he backed off from the casting spot.

After resting the pool for fifteen minutes, Steve and I resumed chumming. We scrambled on hands and knees, edging up to the stalks of grass and no longer grasping at hoppers clinging to stems, but instead snapping the insects accurately onto the stream with a flick of the middle finger.

"Damn," Steve huffed as he crab-walked, "if someone was paying me to work this hard, I'd quit."

The small fish fed more sporadically and never accepted the artificial. Three real hoppers in succession floated over unmolested. "He's probably full," Ken said, but just then the trout sucked down one of those jumbo 1-inch size hoppers.

We suggested various stratagems. "Use a big Muddler, a No. 2," I called. "Let it sink a few inches under."

When Ken hooked the 12-inch fish on the big fly, Steve bounced up with waving arms, "Get the gaff!"

"He's been casting with it," I said.

This brown trout posed as a communal triumph: it was not the biggest fish of the season, but with an investment of nearly an hour of angling time from three fishermen, it definitely ranked as one of the most memorable trout of the year.

Chapter 13

The Effective Imitation
of the Sculpin

THE ATTENDANT at the power-house thrust a finger to sweep along a line of restraining buoys stretching across the Missouri River, "Damn fools take those motor boats in there. Not supposed to do that, of course, but they won't listen. Every year, two or three of them get drowned. Boats chewed up to matchsticks, and then spit out a mile downstream."

Bill Seeples agreed, "It's crazy."

"Fish crazy," the old man said.

"But there are trout down there weighing between 30 and 50 pounds," Seeples explained, the reality of that possibility verified by a 27-pound brown trout caught by a bait caster at Hauser Dam the previous year.

Only four of the dam gates poured water from the lake. The sluice, a narrow ribbon, tumbled in a mere trickle against the mass of cement face. The deceptively pitiful amount of flow veiled the force of the water until it crashed onto the apron in a shattering spew."

In the autumn of a drought-year, migrating brown trout congregated against the barrier of the dam. Fish appeared in slower currents of the spill basin to gorge on bait-minnows crippled and stunned in the fall of the wash. At tongues between the foam of the races, the trout slashed the water in fluries of pursuit.

Seeples scrambled from a perch on a grey hump of stone as he prattled in a run-on tumble of speech, "Now here it is...a giving mood of this river...only thinking that those are mythical monsters cutting up out there."

From an isolated jut below the power grids, we fanned precise casts with shooting-head lines onto the lanes of the river. We plied the bulky deer-hair patterns against the bluster of a wind that swept off the expanse of water, two figures on a sandy spit of beach below a cauldron tangle obscured by hastening dusk.

When I nailed a bouncing 3-pound rainbow, instead of one of those brown trout, I quickly skittered the fish into the net. I slit the stomach lining of the injured trout, squeezing out two sculpins that measured longer than the 3/0 Bullhead pattern.

I mused while I tossed the weighted hook, "Did you ever wonder? Maybe these baby shark attractors aren't big enough?"

Despite the hurry of each cast, our moment of opportunity dwindled. "Be there for us," Seeples muttered.

In the early moments of shadowy twilight, rises of innumerable whitefish and small trout spattered the slicks of the river. Between narrow hills, outlines of scrub trees solidified to silhouettes at the crest of the horizon. The water assumed a more beckoning promise in darkened swirlings of current.

An obliging fish walloped the Bullhead pattern. But then, after the slam of the strike, the trout sank to deeper water in sublime ignorance of the curve of the rod. It moved with an unconcerned sidling against a taut line, yielding none of the extra distance.

All the while Seeples recited a strategy for bigger fish, "Just nag him. Keep him down there — the water runs in one direction there — keep him down there away from hell's own bathtub."

150

But after only ten minutes, the trout broke in an accelerating rush towards the face of the dam. In the churning pools of the gate-mix, the line flexed between fish and angler to twist in pretzel-knots in the upheaval currents. Slack carrying into balls of loose loops signaled loss of the trout.

We beached two more rainbows of 3½ pounds in a cluster of evening strikes. "Are these the monsters?"

In the weakening light, it was difficult to detect the motion of even the orange running line. "Maybe we need harpoons?"

I surrendered for the moment to the futility of flogging the river in random plucks at the edges. I nestled against lingering warmth trapped in the black rocks and popped open a canister of hot soup, as I sat in a reverie of disconsolate solitude.

Seeples persisted against the river. He worked in fishless effort until the last faint light, when he grunted and boomed as he drove the hook, "All right!" — the triumph of an indomitable angler who subdues any odds through will and force of expended energy.

He thrust the rod tip upwards to free the line from the turmoil in the deep water. He pumped to gather backing onto the reel drum. As the head-shaking trout dug vigorously towards the slope of the spit, he held the fish shy of the maelstrom of mixing currents.

That was the struggle — if the fish were stopped on the run, it was always the turning point. Chatter orchestrated the capture, "He's coming to the right."

As we hefted the thrashing trout in cords of the hoop-net, the handle bent with the weight. When we hoisted the jawed male onto the scale, the needle jiggled in the flashlight-shine. Bill huffed, "Almost 7 pounds."

We trundled across the walkway above the dam in an irridescent glare of flood lights. "There were bigger fish than that — fifteen pounds or so — down there tonight."

"There were! We'll just have to keep working until we hit one of those barrel-runners."

During the weeks of a lingering Indian summer of angling, the

152

10 pound mark endured as a barrier. Although we caught a number of fish scaling this level, we never landed a brown trout noticeably over that — the puzzle occupying days of contemplation during empty moments of repetitive casting.

The art of catching a trout over 20 inches involves unique methods, but the techniques are not any more difficult than general practices of the trout quest. The stress is solely on rare moments of vulnerability of a large fish: it is only a different game.

"Here," Seeples boasted, as he snatched up a jar of formaldehyde-soaked sculpins, "here is the grub-ticket for big trout. You finagle a fly with a sculpin-drift, and you'll see how many lunkers there are in a river."

I accepted the offer to learn his way of fishing, "I'll meet you at dawn."

"Be here even a little earlier." He repeated, "You'll catch a trout of over 5 pounds within the week."

The next morning the night air of pre-dawn dark, in a near-freezing chill, was cold enough to send me retreating into the house for a sweater. There was a remembrance, faintly delicious, of early-hour preparations for the opening day ritual of boyhood trout seasons in the East — all at odds with the usual Western practice of not starting to fish a stream before 10:00 a.m.

Bill Seeples was laready waiting at the spot on the Big Hole. He handed me a set-up outfit, a No. 9 glass rod with a floating line oddly spliced with a 12 foot tip of lead-core trolling nylon. On a stubby five foot leader tapered to 1X, there dangled a number 3/0 Bullhead pattern. A tiny bit of fuse wire neatly enwrapped the lowest blood knot of the leader. "Now just watch," he said, as he waded into the rough water.

With that scant instruction and with little understanding of his special outfit or particular technique, I started to fish in the pale light by emulating his probing of each deep slot of the river. I worked the fly upstream and slightly across, shaking loose rolls of

153

line out into the path of the return drift.

While I flogged the water in fishless penitence all morning, he visited me at roughly one-hour intervals. Perching on the bank like a critical vulture, Bill observed with indecipherable grunts — until, each time, he offered another bit of advice on technique. "It's almost the same as steelhead fishing, except that we're matching the habits of the favorite food of these trout. This method works because it puts the fly right on the bottom, where that sculpin lives."

Each time, he cast 25 to 35 feet upstream. He gently stripped in line only as the fly reached a slight angle above the wading position, trailing the drift down-flow with the point of the rod and never pulling the fly off the bottom. As the cast drew abreast, he lifted the rod to control the slack; then, as the fly bounced below, he slowly lowered the rod, bowing and leaning to increase the drift.

At the end of the day, I still stood in the river, shoulders sore from holding the rod in a liberty stance and legs worn from balancing in the current, and yet I fished as diligently as at day-break. I never noticed as Bill approached behind me. "Hey," he hollered, "you just had a strike."

"I never saw it," I protested.

"There," he pointed at the river. "Right in front of you, when the fly was deepest. Sometimes later in the drift, when the fly swims off the bottom, fish hit hard. But right there they just pick it up. Then the line bends back upstream. That's what you watch for."

I noticed, as I studied him fishing, that the drift was not a "dead" process at all. As the Bullhead bounced across from his position, he mended any above-surface slack upstream. All during the float, he drew softly on the rod in a "touch/release" control to make the fly scratch the bottom in feeble nods.

As we quit for the night, he conceded, "I think you're getting the knack."

I grinned with feigned confidence, "I'll be here in the morning."

He added a final dictum of advice, "Anybody can fish when he's catching fish, and that's why most guys go after small trout."

Bill Seeples

The scales are so fine that the sculpin appears smooth-skinned. The pectoral fins are broad and fan-shaped. A bridge of bone extends from the cheek to the eye to form the depressed head. The color-shade is mottled a light or dark spatter of tone to match the rock-blend of the environment.

The sculpin is a bottom-scavenging omnivore. It clings to niches of the bed in pure oxygenated water. In daylight, the weak-swimming fish hides under the stones. When the sculpin is swept off the bottom, it drifts helpless until a sanctuary of rocks is regained. The most vulnerable moments for this nocturnal fish are during maximum movement, dawn and rusk.

155

By the fourth day, the marathon hours of angling no longer passed as an ordeal of endurance. There were still no large fish to my account, but missed strikes and momentary hook-ups enlivened the casting. And during this time, the sense of expectation was growing, as if the reward was assured for work I devoted to the task.

Each day I learned a little more as Seeples doled out hints. "Here, watch this now." He bounced the fly against a sunken stump, which offered one of these horrendous mazes that most fly fishermen pass by after a perfunctory cast. "Now, at this spot here I've lost maybe twenty flies. But I've caught big fish here too. It's a chance worth taking.

"A brown trout will grab a sculpin almost anytime he sees it. But for a fish to see the fly, even if it's acting right, it has to be down at his nose. That's the trouble with most fishermen when they make a presentation to a big-fish spot: not near enough and not deep enough."

In the evening, as I covered a rock-studded run, the sunken line slowed preceptibly in the drift. With a sweeping pull of the left hand on the line and a lift of the right hand on the rod, I connected with the satisfying bulk of something solid, the first fish with the "stutter-twitch."

Seeples helped me scoop out the 6-pound brown trout. "You see, it can't be explained exactly; or even shown. It's a knack — a man has to feel when the fly is creeping. There was nothing that I could tell you."

The "stutter-twitch" was the name of the technique, a delicate draw on the slack. But even more, it was the cessation of pull before the tightening line ever lifted the fly. The "knack" was the knowledge of precisely the correct tension to feather the fly without raising it from the bottom.

I never totally understood what happened to the fly underwater, until I dove with scuba gear. "If there isn't a bullhead-eater down there," I said, "I'll let you know."

On the river bottom, I perched within feet of a trout. In a calmer flow between twin rips of faster current, I held easily next to a crossing shelf, huddling close to the quieter water, where the fish partially hid under a hang of rock in this valley-run.

The fly tumbled into the river 20 feet above the shelf. All the lead-core line fell onto the slow center path, plummeting quickly towards the bottom. After 7 feet of drift, the Bullhead bounced to the level of the rocks. The fly swam sideways in a wobbling stop-and-drop flutter across the stream for 10 feet down the notch, until it swung up into a faster belt of current.

The Bullhead dropped a foot farther down the bed on each meticulous cast. A prime across-stream twitch teased the trout, as the fly hopped nearer the holding position. When the methodic pay-off drift sank precisely at the far end of the shelf, the fish eased forward to inhale the fraudulent prop of the magnificent act of deception.

The trout bolted so fast that it almost crashed into my face mask. It thrashed out in panic fury, never seeking the refuge of the ledge again. It skittered across bands of current at the shallower head of the run to tire quickly.

"Hey," I yelled at Seeples, as I pushed above the surface, "did you know that bull was there?"

"How would I know that?" he grinned.

"That was too beautiful."

"It's braille for the fly fisherman."

The sinking line-tip* cut through the current, and yet it still curled higher in the flow at a pace slightly faster than that of the fly bouncing in the bottom dead-area. Mends of the floating portion of line counter-acted the drag of the swift surface water. Each time, the minimal tension of an aborted draw tightened the leader perceptibly to the keel weight of fuse-wire wrapping, but the inching

---

*The length of this lead-core tip section varies from 8 feet to 25 feet, depending on the depth and swiftenss of the water. For less boisterous trout streams, Hi-density sink-tip lines are satisfactory.

pull of slack into a faster band of upper current scuttled the Bullhead across the rocks.

The quest for a trout of trophy dimensions sets a methodical
task. Often the moments are lonely — but not boring, if the expecta-
tions are worthy. Even a single fish in a day is a fine triumph, if the
trout is a big one. The angler remains alert in the hope of that single
opportunity.

Bill Seeples gave hints on techniques of working for big trout.
He qualified a basic premise, "I start out early in the morning, and I
stay out until late at night. I don't even stop for lunch"; a dedication
that explains why he is so well-known as a big trout fly fisherman.

The knack of this type of angling is to retain enthusiasm over
the fishless hours. With each cast, a Goliath brown is mentally
imagined to rap the fly. The mind of the angler is ever keen for the
moment. The promised fish is always assured on the next cast.

Appendix

*Appendix fly pattern sketches
are by Jeff Johnson;
photos by Glen Zander.*

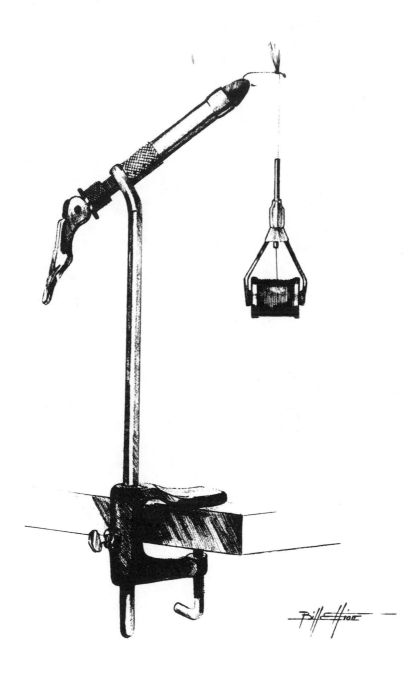

Appendix

Favorite Patterns and Random Notes

By the conditions of his art, the fly fisherman is a superstitious soul. If an angler catches a trout at 2 o'clock on a rainy St. Swithin's Day with a Blue Quill, assuredly the next St. Swithin's Day at 2 o'clock he casts the same pattern. If he catches another trout on the Blue Quill, he is convinced of the fly's specific value. If he encounters an unsuccessful fisherman on the stream, he solemnly metes out advice: "Truly, this is the moment for the Blue Quill."

In defiance of logic, if the pattern fails at similar future circumstances, faith is nevertheless unshaken; for memory has irrevocably bestowed magic on the Blue Quill — and what greater angling secret is there than the confidence of a fisherman?

COLOR THEORY FOR THE FLYTIER

An angler on a stream during the frenzied moment of insect abundance fusses through a myriad assortment of patterns. If the person is a meticulous soul prepared for the crisis, there at stream-side he creates a fly of appropriate color to match the natural. "Now," he announces, "this is it."

To which a skeptic might reply,"Don't believe your own eyes."

It is a fine ritual, indeed, for the studious fly fisherman to hold a natural and an imitation up to the sky to examine the specimens for comparison in the available light, a procedure based on the patent fallacy that trout and man view color in the same perspective.

The natural insect is a vibrant blend of shading, not a monochrome wash. Visible colors of the spectrum combine in impressionistic mixture to lend the tone of dominant hue, but a sticky problem for the flytier exists in the range of visible colors that contribute to the sum effect.

The human eye records color in a wave-length range of between 1/33,000th to 1/67,000th of an inch, but the trout eye additionally perceives color of a lower range in the ultra-violet bands of the spectrum. A trout views a color that is a combination of light-values, but the resultant combo-grouping is different from the color effect that a human eye perceives with the absence of shorter-length bands.

Some colors visible to a trout are invisible to an angler. Viewing a fly against natural light of the sky shows the limit of the spectrum visible to man against a chroma-context of a different background. A possible assumption is that even the sky is a varying shade in the violet-sensitive visual acuity of trout.

Direct rays of the sun act only on translucent portions of an artificial fly. Any color-view of the underside of solid materials of a

162

fly is cast by rays reflected upwards from the streambed. Light bounced off a jumble of rocks spatters the underside of the artificial with a varying speckle of intensity.

Pragmatic anglers of English chalk streams often match a natural insect according to a proven color preference of trout. The body of choice for the imitative pattern of the blue-winged olive *(Ephemerella ignata)* is an orange quill. If the color correlation is not consistent with the perspective of the fisherman, in the evening dim, selective trout nevertheless will choose the fly which appears quite different to the eye of the angler.

Possibly the strongest argument for impressionistic blending of materials of artificial flies is the simple admission that the angler does not always know for certain which color-effect trout perceive as dominant.

In tying patterns to match a natural insect, it is simple to include in the dubbing blend an array of minute particles — wools, fiber acrylics, natural furs — in color specks too small to be particularly noticeable in the final mix. Even in lighter blends of dubbing, it is possible to incorporate fragments of pale green or flourescent orange or mottled brown as bits of fine contrast to the solid intensity of white or cream.

The two-fold benefits of an impressionistic fly are color variegation and color diversity. The varying chromatics of the material add a subtle shading reminiscent of the living insect, hinting at possible tones unseen by an angler. The mix offers multiple color-effects to tempt the selective trout.

DRY FLIES

STANDARD DRY FLY FAVORITES

In angling literature, the dry fly was initially discussed as a complete concept by George R. Pulman in 1851 in the *Vade Mecum of Fly Fishing for Trout,* although the author was not the originator of this angling method. The floating fly undoubtedly was an idea which arrived long before the technology required to produce needed tackle. Even the heavy irons of wet fly patterns were cast to drift the surface momentarily, but the full-blown dry fly method was probably born with the advent of fine light-wire hooks.

Gray Coughlin

This obscure pattern is a color cross between an Adams and a Hare's Ear. It is as effective as this justly touted pair of standards; the Gray Coughlin is an all-around dry fly for a typical trout stream.

> *Hook:* Mustad-Viking 94840 (extra fine wire)
> *Tail:* medium dun rooster hackle fibers
> *Body:* greyish brown Hare's Ear dubbing (guard hairs untrimmed)
> *Wing:* matched sections of grey-slate duck quill
> *Hackle:* brown rooster hackle/grizzly rooster hackle (mixed)

165

Housatonic Quill

This is a popular dry fly on the Housatonic River of Connecticut, a fine subtle variation of the Quill Gordon or Hendrickson. The thin silhouette of the quill body is especially effective at dusk in imitating the opaque evening appearance of the mayfly.

Hook:	Mustad-Viking 94840 (extra fine wire)
Tail:	grey badger rooster hackle fibers
Body:	striped peacock quill (a quill with pronounced light bands)
Wing:	speckled wood duck (dyed mandarin)
Hackle:	grey badger rooster hackle

Leadwing Coachman

This darker version of the standard Coachman is a fly with a special purpose in my angling method, a pattern I find effective at shade-spots of a trout stream. I stalk the water on a sunny day, placing the Leadwing Coachman under hanging bushes or among trailing snags to fool stray trout, which seem to laze at the cool niches even during the mid-summer months.

Hook:	Mustad-Viking 94840 (extra fine wire)
Tail:	coachman brown rooster hackle fibers
Body:	peacock herl
Wing:	matched sections of grey-slate duck quill
Hackle:	coachman brown rooster hackle

Pink Lady

This was the original pattern of George LaBranche; it is a sunshine fly for casting bright and bouncing water.

Hook: Mustad-Viking 94840 (extra fine wire)
Tail: ginger rooster hackle fibers
Body: pink floss
Rib: gold tinsel
Wing: matched sections of light slate duck quill
Hackle: ginger rooster hackle

Light Cahill

In early and middle days of summer, cream mayflies burst into prominence on a stream. Each evening, the straw duns emerge to train fish into a pattern of selectivity. For the space of a month, the Light Cahill is the most valuable standard dry fly in a fly fisherman's box.

Hook: Mustad-Viking 94840 (extra fine wire)
Tail: ginger rooster hackle fibers
Body: red fox belly fur (cream)
Wing: wood duck (dyed mandarin)
Hackle: cream rooster hackle

Pale Evening Dun (Charles Fox)

This fly was patterned for a specific insect of the spring creeks of Pennsylvania — *Ephemerella dorothea;* but any fly, to attain universal appeal, requires a more general imitative quality. The Pale Evening Dun encompasses broad groups of ubiquitous olive-sulphur mayflies that proliferate in rich stream habitats. On any day in mid-summer on the Western spring-creeks, the Dun simulates the important pale-shade *Baetis* or *Ephemerella* or *Pseudocloeon* that parade on slick flows in dependable procession.

167

> *Hook:* Mustad-Viking 94840 (extra fine wire)
> *Tail:* honey rooster hackle fibers/pale blue grey
> rooster hackle fibers (mixed)
> *Body:* pale green fur dubbing
> *Wing:* grey mallard fibers
> *Hackle:* honey rooster hackle/pale blue grey hackle (mixed)

A SERIES OF TRUDE PATTERNS

The Trude series of down-wing patterns, a versatile type of dry fly, were the forerunners of all the current hair-wing dry variations. Historically effective on Western rivers, initially as a wet fly, the type simulates the stone fly and caddis fly silhouette; later hair-wing imitations derive from these patterns.

A memorandum of Carter Harrison notes the genesis of Trude patterns:

> In September of 1901, I was camping with friends on the Big Spring branch of the Snake River in Idaho, a few miles below where the stream — at least 100 feet wide and flowing with a good current close to 2 feet deep — bubbles out of the ground in a group of springs that cover a quarter of an acre.
> Mr. A. S. Trude, who was in residence at his Algenia Ranch, heard of our presence, came in our absence with a couple of sheep-wagons, took down tents and packed up our belongings. When we got back to camp, he was on the spot to move us bag and baggage to his ranch, 20 miles distant. We compromised on camping in his barnyard.
> During our 4-day stay, there was a constant jocular dispute between Graham H. Harris, an angler of sorts, who not only tied his trout

and salmon flies, but made split bamboo rods of the first quality, and myself and Mr. Trude, as to the proper size of flies to be used on the river, a stream of water so clear that, looking ahead when wading, one could not tell whether it was 18 inches or 4 feet deep! Mr. Trude felt that a No. 10 or No. 8 fly was in order on it — we clung to salmon flies on No. 4 hooks.

For years, I had tied my own flies. In my outfit was a large hook which, from time to time when fishing for muskellonge, I had lashed to wood to make a gaff. The night before breaking camp, we were in the ranch library, reading and gossiping, when Mr. Trude left the room. A queer notion came into my head. I got out the big hook. A red spaniel was lying on the rug. I clipped a bunch of hair from his flank. The rug was roughly woven, with a lot of red worsted in it. I clipped enough to tie a body on the hook. On impulse, I tied the dog-hair as a wing and fashioned over it a sort of hackle of red squirrel-hair. When Mr. Trude returned, I got up on the table and, in a flapdoodle speech, thanked him for his invariable kindness during the days we had spent on his place, ending with the statement that, to show our appreciation, I had tied a small fly for his use in future fishing and further to honour him, I had named the fly the "A. S. Trude!"

Looking it over, the thing looked so darned good that I got out regular fly-tying material and tied two flies on No. 4 hooks, one with a red yarn body wrapped with silver tinsel, using squirrel tail hair for the wing and a red rooster hackle tied over it, the other unchanged except for green yarn supplanting the red.

The next morning, when Edw. B. Ellicott and I set out to fish the Buffalo some miles above the Trude Ranch, Mr. Trude asked us to bring in all the fish we caught — it was late in the season; he wanted to salt them down for winter use of his help. We took turn and turn about fishing the creek; Ellicott would fish two bends following me; catching up, he would go ahead two bends with me following. At each bend there was a deep hole and in the clear crystal water we could see large cutthroat trout lazily waving tails at the bottom. To our offerings, scant attention was paid. Once, when Ellicott passed me, I remembered the Trude fly, put on the red-bodied sample; when I caught up with him I had 5 large trout in the creel. He saw them, learned the fly I had used and offered $5.00 for it — begged me to sell! I gave him the green-bodied Trude.

That evening at the ranch, we emptied two creels, large ones, too; the creels and the side and back pockets of our hunting coats were all filled to overflowing. *

*This excerpt is included in a section quoted in *Fly Tying*, by William Sturgis.

The prolific professional flytier from Chicago, Benjamin Winchell, supplied well-to-do sportsmen of the early decades of the century. He touted the Trude fly, spreading its reputation and selling so many of a green-bodied variation that in the popular fishing regions of eastern Canada a dry fly version acquired the title of Quebec Trude.

Red Trude (wet fly version)

Hook:	Mustad-Sproat 3906
Thread:	black 4/0 nylon
Body:	red wool
Rib:	silver tinsel
Wing:	red squirrel hair
Hackle:	brown rooster hackle (collar)

Black Trude (dry fly version)

Hook:	Mustad-Viking 94840
Thread:	black 4/0 nylon
Tail:	black rooster hackle fibers
Body:	black spun fur
Rib:	silver tinsel
Wing:	black kip tail hair
Hackle:	black rooster hackle

Quebec Trude (dry fly version)

Hook:	Mustad-Viking 94840
Thread:	black 4/0 nylon
Tail:	scarlet rooster hackle fibers
Body:	green spun fur
Rib:	gold tinsel
Wing:	grey squirrel hair
Hackle:	brown rooster hackle

O'Connor Rio Grande King

The hair-wing version of the standard Rio Grande King is often linked with the name of Richard J. "Dick" O'Connor. The angler from Denver is one of the premier trophy-trout fly fishermen in the country. He annually catches trout in the 7 to 14-lb. class, prize winning fish in the Field & Stream contest. He casts this Trude variation exclusively to meticulously stalked and marked trout — a specialist using only a single pattern.

Hook:	Mustad-Sproat 3906 (regular wire)
Thread:	black 4/0 nylon
Tail:	golden pheasant tippet fibers
Body:	black chenille
Wing:	white kip tail hair
Hackle:	brown rooster hackle

The flies of the Trude series are valuable on the riffle structure of a trout stream, but there are two Trude patterns I tie especially for the chop-water. I use the very fine hair of Monga Ring-Tail for the wing on these flies. The absorbant hair is worked with enough paste floatant to support the pattern on the surface in a delicate drift. The white wing spreads in the meniscus to provide visibility for both trout and angler. On the false air-cast, the Ring-Tail hair retains sufficient moisture — in contrast to the water shedding kip tail — to pull the fly off a high ride on hackle points.

The color-choice of these attractor patterns is based on visibility against a non-complementing background. Brown or red are distinct against the filtered spectrum of a clear sky; black or cream are identifiable against the muted reflection of a cloudy sky — a Royal Trude is a favorite sunshine fly, and a Lady Heather is a select overcast fly.

APPENDIX

Royal Trude

Hook:	Mustad-Viking 94840
Thread:	black 6/0 nylon
Body:	scarlet floss (center joint)
Rear Butt:	peacock herl
Forward Butt:	peacock herl
Wing:	white Monga Ring-Tail hair
Hackle:	coachman brown hackle
Tail:	coachman brown rooster hackle fibers

Lady Heather

In Montana the sky cues from the land and carries an illusion of vastness. The sky dominates either with a sharp blue of sun or with a shifting grey of clouds, and in streaks during fall or spring especially, the gloom days of grey linger. A weak light plays over the already changeable sparkle on the water, and a fly drifting among the flecks of foam and bits of debris disappears on the riffle chop, bedeviling the angler with futile eye strain.

Grey days are not rare, and they are a blessing since in the minimal light intensity trout range boldly throughout the daytime hours. Then trout stack in the riffles, alert to items drifting suspended in the flow or perched on the surface, and they forage with quick stabs out of protected pockets to snatch passing food from the current.

On a grey day, the Lady Heather is a fine fly to pop onto rough water. The white wing is distinct to the angler and not too difficult to follow on the drift. The cream of the thin body is a visual entity to the trout; and yet in overall color-pattern, the fly is not too monochromatic for fish-sight, which is so keen on a muted day. The grey and grizzly hackle-blend is a broken image speckle against the background, color-true enough to portray opaque parts of an insect without the false image of solid bulk.

172

Hook: Mustad-Viking 94840
Thread: black 6/0 nylon
Tail: dark blue dun hackle fibers
Butt: grey muskrat fur (dubbed)
Body: cream spun fur (wrapped)
Wing: white Monga Ring-Tail hair
Hackle: grizzly/dark blue dun (mixed)

TYING INSTRUCTIONS FOR ROYAL TRUDE
(Low-Profile/Attractor)

Thread: black — or add a distinctive touch by using
unwaxed red thread glossed at the
head with varnish.
Tail: brown hackle fibers with high quality stiffness
(not overly long)

Use only a few hackle fibers properly spread to balance the fly on the water. A thick bunch of fibers is ineffective in floating a fly because the water mats the mass into a sodden lump.

To spread the fibers, after attaching the tail, lift them and wrap the thread three times close to the base. One or two further wraps on top of the fibers will spread the individual strands along the platform.

Rear butt: 3 strands of peacock herl

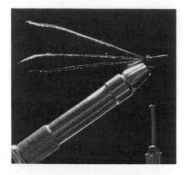

The first part of a Royal Trude to be ruined is the herl, which is quickly chopped by the teeth of a fish. To make the herl butts more secure, wrap the herl clockwise around the thread and proceed to wind the covered thread around the hook shank until the butt is formed.

1. Pull the herl down and grasp it in the right hand.
2. Pass the herl across to the left hand.
3. Complete a wind around the thread in a clock-wise manner by passing the herl in back from the right hand to the left hand.
4. Wrap enough herl around the thread for the winding of the rear butt.

Center Joint: red floss

After winding the first butt on the shank, leave excess of the strands of herl unwrapped.

1. Tie in the floss.
2. Run the thread forward with the herl pinioned flat on top of the shank.
3. Cover the thread and herl with wraps of the center section of red floss.
4. Tie down and clip off the excess floss.

Forward Butt: peacock herl — with the same strands that
formed the rear butt

1. Wrap the herl clock-wise around the
   thread.

2. Wrap the covered thread around the
   shank to form the butt.

3. Clip off the excess herl.

(It is a personal preference, but I make the
forward butt slightly smaller than the rear
butt.)

Wing: white hair

Kip tail hair is frequently used for a down-wing fly, but for a neater
appearance of the Trude, I use Monga Ring-Tail hair. Make sure the
Monga is worked through with a sparse application of Mucilin to make the
fine hair water repellant.

1. Tie in the wing hair to extend to the
   bend of the hook; the clump of hair not
   overly thick, but spread by building a
   base of thread underneath.

2. Clip the excess hair butts in a taper to
   the front.

3. Place a drop of cement on the butts of
   hair to secure the tie.

175

Hackle: coachman brown rooster hackle of high quality

Two hackle feathers are wound on the shank of the hook, but they are applied reverse of the usual Eastern tying procedure. The hackles are tied down with the dull side facing forward. They are wrapped around the shank in this manner.

When they are wrapped with the reverse method, the fibers of the feather assume a forward cant. With the hackle position naturally set, the fibers resist collapsing to the rear as the fly is drifted on fast water..

Whip finish and cement the head to complete the fly.

FORE AND AFT DRY FLIES

The simple bi-hackle fly represents an old English style, and in modern dress this version, renamed the Renegade, is one of the most commercially popular dry patterns in the Northwest region. Several variations — Rascal, Outlaw, Knave — have been adapted by flytier Dixon Renner and are also growing in popularity in areas of Wyoming and Idaho.

176

Renegade

Fore Hackle:	white rooster hackle
Aft Hackle:	brown rooster hackle
Body:	peacock herl
Tip:	gold tinsel (narrow)

Knave

Fore Hackle:	cream rooster hackle
Aft Hackle:	cream rooster hackle
Body:	brown fur dubbing
Tip:	gold tinsel (narrow)

Outlaw

Fore Hackle:	silver badger rooster hackle
Aft Hackle:	silver badger rooster
Body:	black fur dubbing
Tip:	silver tinsel (narrow)

Rascal

Fore Hackle:	white rooster/ grizzly rooster (mix)
Aft Hackle:	brown rooster/ grizzly rooster (mix)
Body:	yellow fur dubbing
Tip:	silver tinsel (narrow)

(The tip is wound behind the rear hackle. The tinsel serves to prevent the hackle wrap from slipping down the bend of the hook shank.)

177

KOLZER FIREFLIES — A TOUCH OF FLOURESCENCE

Visibility is a two-edged sword — at moments an effect to achieve or at moments an effect to avoid. Black or white are colors which stand out against a background of faint sky. Flourescent tints are radiant shades which retain color-value in reduced light.

Flourescent dye-colors add a note of identity to a fly. For the standard trout pattern, the day-bright hues are possibly most effective if the materials are used sparingly, but in faded light of evening or in limits of muddy water, radiant colors maximize the available illumination.

The Kolzer dry-patterns are popular in the West, but with them I also experienced a fine flurry of action one evening with brawling rainbows on the Lamoille River of Vermont.

Kolzer Orange

Hook:	Mustad-Viking 7957-B (long shank)
Thread:	black 5/0 nylon
Tail:	brown bucktail hair
Palmer Hackle:	brown rooster hackle
Body:	orange gantron (flourescent)
Wing:	brown bucktail hair
Front Hackle:	brown rooster hackle

178

Kolzer Yellow

Hook:	Mustad-Viking 7957-B (long shank)
Thread:	black 5/0 nylon
Tail:	brown bucktail hair
Palmer Hackle:	brown rooster hackle
Body:	yellow gantron (flourescent)
Wing:	brown bucktail hair
Front Hackle:	brown rooster hackle

CADDIS FLY PATTERNS

TYING INSTRUCTIONS FOR THE CADDIS PUPA

Grannom Pupa *(Brachycentrus)*

Hook: Mustad-Viking 94840 (extra fine wire)

Both weighted and unweighted versions of this pattern are tied on extra fine dry fly steel for better hooking penetration.

Bend the hook ¾ of the way up the shank into a slight down-curve.

For the weighted fly:

1. Lacquer the thread-wrapped shank.

2. Fasten the piece of lead wire to the underside of the hook, leaving the eye and the bend of the hook clear.

Thread: brown 6/0 nylon

179

Overbody: dark brown Sparkle* yarn

1. Separate one ply from the 4-ply yarn.
2. Completely fray one end of the yarn piece with a needle.
3. Spread the strands sparsely on top of the hook shank.
4. Tie down the strands at the bend of the hook.
5. Trim the stubs.

Repeat the procedure — tie down strands of a second ply of yarn to the bottom side of the hook bend.

(The simulation of the pupal sheath is achieved with a very sparse film of overbody material enveloping the underbody.)

Underbody: dubbing mix of dark speckle of Hare's Ear and dark brown Sparkle

In the pupal series the imitative effect is accomplished with an impressionistic blend of two parts of fur (usually the darker shade) and one part of yarn. The translucence of the fur and the glisten of the yarn show through the sparse threads of the overbody.

1. Dub the blend onto the thread.
2. Wind the body ¾ of the way up the shank.
3. Pick out the thin underbody to make it shaggy.

---

*The generic term "Sparkle" is used to identify bright yarn, but the material is available under different brand names in most discount centers — colors are obtainable in one brand or another.

Forming the complete body:

1. Pull the strands of the overbody forward (not drawn tight, but left enveloping the underbody).

2. Separate the strands (individual filaments) to spread completely.

3. Tie down in front of the underbody — fasten the top strands around the top of the shank and the bottom strands around the bottom of the shank to encircle the hook.

   (Simple sparseness is an invaluable virtue in a wet fly.)

Legs: dark grouse fibers

The wing slats that lie alongside the natural pupa are omitted in the imitation. The stiff quills extending along the sides detract from the color vibrancy of the fly.*

Hackle ragged fibers around the shank to sweep backwards.

Head: dark brown marabou fibers

1. Tie in 4 or 5 strands of marabou
2. Wrap the strands clock-wise onto the thread (forming a rope).
3. Wind the cover thread to the eye.

   Whip finish with a small tie-off.

---

*In pupal specimens recovered from the gullet of a fish, the pre-formed wings are a distinct color-block, the enveloping sheath of the insect dissolved by stomach acid; possibly this explains the side slats of past imitations.

Wings of the live-swimming insect fold inside the pupal sac. The outline of the form is obscured in the glitter of air. In the artificial pattern, the opaque slats of duck-primary screen the natural radiance of the Sparkle filaments.

THE EMERGENT CADDIS — A USEFUL MODIFICATION

Early during the testing of caddis patterns, a need was apparent for a fly to match the emerging insect at the moment between the pupa in the water and the adult in the air. The half-unfolded wings and the partially unloosened sheath were simulated in a surface-film fly adopting characteristics of the experimental patterns for both pupa and adult. The pupal pattern and the adult pattern were subsequently altered, but the effective Emergent Caddis remained virtually unchanged from the original trial-fly of five years ago.

The unweighted emergent fly imitates the caddis during the final struggle from the shuck. The pattern is fished with a feeble drift and twitched at the end of the swing. The fly is dubbed more roughly with a mix of longer strands of fur. Filaments of the dazzle sheath are unevenly frayed to hang freely to represent the loosening skin. The wing of deer body hair anchors the "damp" fly in the surface-film.*

TYING INSTRUCTIONS FOR THE FLUTTERING CADDIS

This pattern type is the basic Fluttering Caddis version prescribed by Leonard Wright, Jr. — with minor variations of tying technique for a smoother skittering motion of the active fly. These recommended correlations with the naturals include a wing of stiff mink-tail hairs and a hackle of a "spider" winding.

---

*J. Marshall Edmonds proposed an interesting theory on the Emergent Caddis: "I realize that it is meant for the emergence of the pupa (when it works superbly), but with the strands of Sparkle hanging off the back, it might also represent the fallen egg-laying female. That straggle of yarn catches light and looks like the air pushed into the water as the adult struggles. Just an idea, but the fly knocks them dead during the brush hatch, also. It's the only universal caddis pattern."

182

Spotted Sedge *(Hydropsyche)*

    Hook: Mustad-Viking 94833 (3X fine wire)
Thread: brown 6/0 nylon (unwaxed thread)

      Wind the thread slightly down the bend.

    Body: dubbing of straw-yellow rabbit fur

1. Dub the sparse application of fine fur onto the tying thread.
2. Wrap a thin body of fur evenly 2/3 of the way up the shank.
3. Wind the thread at tie-off in a base built up level to the body material.

    Wing: medium brown hair fibers of mink tail

      Without a tail on the fly, it is important that wing fibers are long enough on the Fluttering pattern to raise the hook point off the water surface.

1. Clip the stiff guard hairs from the tail of the mink (pull away the soft dubbing at the base of the fibers).
2. Even out the loose tips.
3. Position the bunch flat over the top of the hook shank with the hair tips extending back beyond the bend — fibers spread on a level plane to balance the fly on the water.
4. Bind the hair down with firm wraps.
5. Snip the hair butts at a tapering slant.
6. Cement the butts.

(Wright recommends tying the wing with three applications of rooster spade-hackle fibers — two of the bunches positioned at each side of the shank to form a tube shape.)

Hackle: 2 cock hackle feathers — stiff and glossy

The feathers are tied (in the manner of a skating spider) to keep the outside circumference of the hackle wrap on a narrow edge for a smooth skitter.

1st hackle – golden badger rooster hackle

1. Tie in the feather with the glossy side facing to the rear.

2. Wind the feather with close neat wraps.

3. With thumb and fore-finger jam the spacing of the wraps tightly to the rear.

4. Tie down — snip the excess tip.

2nd hackle – grizzly rooster hackle

1. Tie in the feather with the dull side facing the rear.

2. Wind the feather with close neat wraps (no overlap).

3. Jam the spacing of the wraps tightly to the rear.

4. Tie down — snip the excess tip.

Whip finish and cement the head.

CORRELATION WITH THE NATURALS
(5 GENERA OF CADDIS)

The following descriptions of the habits of the major genera are based on underwater scuba-observation of the life-stages of each insect:

Brachycentrus (Grannom)

Species of this important genus inhabit cold and swift trout streams throughout the continent. Colonies of the distinctive rectangular-chimney larval cases cluster on the stones and sticks of riffle stretches. Populations exist in prolific density in flows of both alkaline and acidic high-nutrient waters.

Upon emergence, the pupae swim neither as strongly nor as rapidly as other caddis species. The insects often wash in momentary struggle just under the surface in fast water until pushed to quieter eddies of the river — an imitation tied on an unweighted light wire hook is often a deadly simulation of the shuck-encumbered pupa.

The brush-hatch of returning adults triggers a frenzy of selective feeding. The mated females splat to the water surface, skittering across or up against the current to enable the water force to strip the greenish mass of eggs from the abdomen.*

------

*An authority of British Isle entomology, Martin Mosely, speculated that the adult female of the species *Brachycentrus subnubilus* crawls down the stems of reeds to lay the eggs.

185

Grannom Pupa

Hook:	Mustad-Viking 94840 (extra fine wire); 10, 12, 14
Thread:	brown 6/0 nylon
Overbody:	chocolate brown Sparkle yarn
Underbody:	blend of dark speckle of Hare's Ear and chocolate brown Sparkle
Hackle:	dark grouse fibers (speckled grey/brown)
Head:	dark brown marabou strands

Emergent Grannom

Hook:	Mustad-Viking 94840; 12, 14
Thread:	brown 6/0 nylon
Overbody:	chocolate brown Sparkle yarn (partially frayed)
Underbody:	olive/brown rabbit fur blend
Wing:	brown speckled tips of deer body hair (spread over the back)
Head:	dark brown marabou strands

The upper Clark Fork below the mouth of spring-run Lost Creek is a prime angling spot for late July. On the gravel of shallow slopes, cases of the grannom crust in such thickness that feet of a wading fisherman crunch with each step. In the evening, the insect adults beat upriver in sheets of advance that obscure a person a few yards away on the stream.

Grannom Adult (Fluttering Caddis)

Hook:	Mustad-Viking 94833 (3X fine wire); 14, 16
Thread:	brown 6/0 nylon
Body:	olive/brown rabbit fur (yellow/green egg sac optional for imitation of the female)
Wing:	brown mink tail hair fibers
Hackle	rear — dark blue dun rooster hackle
(2 feather):	front — grizzly rooster hackle

Leptocella (White Miller)

The imitation of the adult miller is a fine pattern to skip on the flats of a trout stream at night. Success of the general white fluttering simulation is not difficult to explain: the white is a visible color, the shape is a match for moths or other caddis flies, the movement is an attracting action.

The numerous millers dally strictly in a nocturnal setting. The adults dance in gathering masses, sidling above the water. In a cadence of flight, insect concentrations remain above the river, females laying the eggs with quick surface touches that afford the trout little chance at active insects.

The fact that the pattern matching the *Leptocella* often succeeds is true; the fact that trout seldom capture adult millers is also true. The white Fluttering Caddis is an optimum choice for dark-time angling, often better than a dead-drift upwing pattern since the fly is twitched upriver to provide the touch-control of a nearly taut line.

White Miller Adult

Hook:	Mustad-Viking 94833 (3X fine wire); 14, 16
Thread:	pale green 6/0 nylon
Body:	pale green rabbit fur
Wing:	white mink tail hair
Hackle	rear — silver badger rooster hackle
(2 feather):	front — grizzly rooster hackle (light barred markings)

187

The curved sand case of this caddis resembles the horn of a cow. In typically swift currents colonies of the insect cling amid the rubble mix on the swept portions of the stones. This genus proliferates in sandy areas of a trout stream.

The specific pupal imitation of the *Leptocella* is important for early rising fly fishermen in summer. Trout respond to the kicking swim of the fly, which imitates the natural pupae most often found in stomach samples from early morning fish. The angler at dawn encounters the straggling insects of the night emergence.

White Miller Pupa

Hook:	Mustad-Viking 94840; 12, 14, 16
Thread:	pale green 6/0 nylon
Overbody:	white Sparkle yarn
Underbody:	pale greyish green fur dubbing/ pale yellow Sparkle yarn dubbing
Hackle:	mallard breast feather fibers
Head:	straw-yellow marabou fibers

White Miller Emergent

Hook:	Mustad-Viking 94840; 14, 16
Thread:	pale green 6/0 nylon
Overbody:	white Sparkle yarn
Underbody:	pale green rabbit fur
Wing:	cream speckled tips of deer body hair
Head:	straw-yellow marabou fibers

Psilotreta (Dark Blue Sedge)

On classic Adirondack streams, this insect emerges in mid-June, and in this historic setting, the event is seldom unmentioned in fly fishing literature. Preston Jennings notes of the species *Psilotreta frontalis,* "In company with the large mayfly known as the Green Drake,comes a caddis fly which is sometimes taken by the trout in preference to the Green Drake."

This sedge is a despair to the angler as it replaces the preferable surface action of mayflies. It is another pupa of moderate swim-motion. The fish gorge on the sub-surface stage with swirl rises that hump the water. The action deceptively resembles a dry fly spree; and all the worse, the emergence dominates the prime angling hours of a stream.

The emergent pattern serves as an effective simulation of the floundering adult wallowing along helpless in the surface film. The fly is cast upstream in the manner of a greased nymph, the line of drift intercepting a specific rising rish — an art closely akin to the dry fly technique.

Dark Blue Sedge Pupa

Hook:	Mustad-Viking 94840; 10, 12, 14
Thread:	brown 6/0 nylon
Overbody:	chocolate brown Sparkle yarn
Underbody:	black fur dubbing / medium brown Sparkle yarn dubbing
Hackle:	grey speckled grouse fibers
Head:	black marabou fibers

189

Emergent Dark Blue Sedge

Hook:	Mustad-Viking 94840; 12, 14
Thread:	brown 6/0 nylon
Overbody:	chocolate brown Sparkle yarn
Underbody:	dark brown rabbit fur
Wing:	grey tips of deer body hair (dyed)
Head:	black marabou fibers

Adults linger up to two weeks near the stream. The insects fly all day under bridges or beneath bushes over shaded bits of water. With a stray gust of wind, the erratic sedges flop to the current to flit in a hopping dance about the surface.

A fluttering imitation of the adult proves valuable as a searching fly. The subtle twitch at a selected spot excites nearby trout. The ploy of successive casts over a precise lane of current draws fish to rise to the life-like motion of the caddis pattern.

Dark Blue Sedge Adult

Hook:	Mustad-Viking 94833; 12, 14, 16
Thread:	brown 6/0 nylon
Body:	rusty brown rabbit fur
Wing:	bronze grey mink tail fibers
Hackle	rear — bronze blue dun rooster hackle
(2 feather):	front — grizzly rooster hackle

Hydropsyche (Spotted Sedge)

The ecosystem of the typical trout stream in a civilized America is not the same as 30 years ago. Organic sewage and phosphorous leach from the septic clutter of suburbia and agricultural lands drain nitrogen-based components of fertilizer, to enrich bordering streams and rivers. The nutrient increase causes replacement of the once-dominant mayfly with filter-feeding caddis species.*

The fragile mayflies have been diminished; former blizzard emergences of duns are sparse. But now caddis flies are more prevalent on many rivers — always important on rich watersheds anyway — and the most important insect genus for the fly fisherman on many trout streams is the spotted sedge.

This caddis is a net-spinning insect. The larva constructs a silken snare with a wide mouth upstream to face the flow, the base anchored to an object in a riffle. The caddis positions itself at the rear of the tube to gather entrapped algae and organisms supplied by the current.

The larva builds no permanent case until the start of pupation, a period of metamorphosis in a sand hut that lasts 10 to 15 days. The pupa then cuts free through the grated weave at the mouth of the shelter. Misformed cripples often entangle in the silk mesh to sweep away along the bottom. Even able emergents drift with the current momentarily in a stupor before kicking into a swim to the surface.

Fish feed on these pupae at a specific level. Large trout stack at the inflow currents of pools, with noses to the bottom to pick off struggling prey. The fish sidle back and forth to snatch shimmering pupae that sparkle with daylight brightness.

Even in relatively shallow water, an angler casts a fly with a sink-tip line to emulate the vulnerable deep drift of the caddis. The fisherman mends quick curves with the floating portion of the line to moderate the pattern-swing into a gentle pulse along the stream bed — the precise "touch" of the wet fly fisherman that is so deadly for brute trout.

------

*A delicate balance of organic sewage even helps to produce larger trout.

Spotted Sedge Pupa

Hook:	Mustad-Viking 94840; 12, 14
Thread:	brown 6/0 nylon
Overbody:	russet Sparkle yarn
Underbody:	russet Sparkle yarn dubbing / brown fur dubbing
Hackle:	lemon woodduck fibers
Head:	brown marabou strands

Emergent Spotted Sedge

Hook:	Mustad-Viking 94840; 12, 14
Thread:	light brown 6,0 nylon
Overbody:	russet Sparkle yarn
Underbody:	light brown rabbit fur
Wing:	light speckled tips of deer body hair
Head:	brown marabou strands

The Dinky Spotted Sedge is the best dry fly caddis. Masses of the sedge beat upriver, and the females lunge to the current. Skipping take-offs of the insects from the water excite trout out of proportion to the quantity of downed fare. Even in mid-day, unregimented dips of individuals trigger eruptions of greedy rises; until the flurry peaks at early dusk with the magnificent chaos of skating, intermingling falls of caddis carpet the water, luring behemoth trout to the surface.

Spotted Sedge Adult

Hook:	Mustad-Viking 94833
Thread:	light brown 6/0 nylon
Body:	straw-yellow rabbit fur
Wing:	medium brown mink tail fibers
Hackle	rear — golden badger rooster hackle
(2 feather):	front — grizzly rooster hackle

Rhyacophila (Green Caddis)

This caddis is a tease to the innocent angler. Emergence of the pupa triggers the visible fish-frenzy of the slashing rise. Amid a carnival of feeding, a fisherman drifts pretty casts, only to have the dry fly presentation ignored by the majority of trout.

The pupae of the Green Caddis are exceptionally strong and agile swimmers, and the path of emergence is pocked with little hesitation. The insect reaches the surface to burst into the air so quickly it is doubtful if larger trout waste much energy on this active fare.

The feeding fish key to the insect's rapid swim, the trout often flopping into the air in the futile haste of rash pursuit. The activity increases in intensity as more of the pupal specimens pop out all afternoon in advance of the major emergence of late evening.

Feeding on the pupal life-stage is focused not on the surface at all. A trout positions itself at the downstream edge of a riffle. The rise-action is a slashing upwards race to intercept insect, a fish torpedoing in a very different manner from its rise to a slower species of pupa, when a trout breaks through to capture a surface-hesitant insect in the meniscus.

Green Caddis Pupa

Hook:	Mustad-Viking 94840; 12, 14
Thread:	green 6/0 nylon
Overbody:	medium olive Sparkle yarn
Underbody:	dubbing blend of olive Sparkle yarn (⅓) and medium green acryllic fur (⅔) — (marketed under the hobby name "Craft Fur" — a material of intense green chroma to match the coloration of the natural)
Hackle:	grouse fibers (speckled brown)
Head:	brown marabou strands

193

Emergent Green Caddis

Hook:	Mustad-Viking 94840; 12, 14
Thread:	green 6/0 nylon
Overbody:	medium olive Sparkle yarn
Underbody:	green rabbit fur
Wing:	dark speckled tips of deer body hair
Head:	brown marabou strands

The dry fly is not exclusively important as an imitation of the adult insect. Instead of inevitably falling to the surface of the flow, the female crawls under at the downstream face of a rock to paste a sticky mass of eggs to an object, a hesitant ritual, with the insect touching the water-line a few times before the descent.

An appropriate wet fly is the prime imitation of a drowned female that has failed to return safely to the surface. The pattern is cast to drift at the eddies and the edges of spots where trout feed on gathered naturals — this wet fly deceit once produced a beautiful 19-inch hen brown from little Lolo Creek in Montana.

Green Caddis Adult (Wet Fly)

Green Olive (a simple pattern listed in "Flies" by J. Edson Leonard)

Hook:	Mustad-Sproat 3906; 12, 14
Thread:	black 5/0 nylon
Body:	dark olive-green wool
Rib:	fine oval silver tinsel
Wing:	brown mallard fibers
Hackle:	dark olive hen hackle (sparse collar)

Green Caddis Adult (Fluttering Caddis)*

Hook:	Mustad-Viking 94833; 12, 14
Thread:	green 6/0 nylon
Body:	green/tan rabbit fur
Wing:	brown mink tail fibers

---

*The popular Henryville is another effective imitation of the post-mating male and female adults that fall to the surface.

Hackle   rear — medium olive rooster hackle
(2 feather): front — grizzly rooster hackle

Most species of caddis either build a case or weave a silken net, where a sedentary larva hides relatively secure in its restricted life-habit. Artificial imitations of these insects are of dubious value. Naturals are scraped off rocks and sticks by trout, but it is not feasible for a fly fisherman to simulate this inert prey in a moving stream.

The immature stage of the Green Sedge is an exception to the general practice. This larva is an indiscriminate omnivore, which roams free over the riffle clutter of a river bed. Trout feed heavily on the clambering form; not usually to a selective extent, but with a preference so that the contents of a stomach sample may contain 70% or 80% of a mash of "green worms."

The weighted imitation of the caseless caddis is a fine searching pattern for a nymph fisherman. The fly is fished to bounce dead-drift close to the bottom, imitating a familiar sight to foraging trout. It is a fly for the chilled water of late spring, when the insect population of a stream attains maximum density in the weeks prior to the pupation period.

Green Caddis Larva

Hook:	Mustad-Viking 9671 (2X long); 12, 14, 16
Thread:	black 6/0 nylon
Body:	dubbing of olive fur (½) and
(¾ of rear)	green acrylic Craft Fur (½)
Thorax:	dubbing of dark speckled Hare's Ear (½)
(¼ of front)	and green acrylic fur (½)
Ribbing:	stripped quill of a brown rooster hackle (to prevent splitting of the quill, soak it for ½ hour in water before winding)
Hackle:	dark speckled grouse fibers (tied under in a ragged spread to the rear)

NOTES ON THE HENRYVILLE

The Henryville, an older palmered hackle down-wing, is an alternative pattern for imitating the action of adult caddis. At moments, this fly is more effective for raising selective fish than the Fluttering Caddis. With more hackle points pressing on the surface film, the Henryville palmer radiates a greater shower of light indentations, presenting a more realistic illusion of motion on the upstream dead-drift.

To shed light on the history of the Henryville Special, the following quotation is a paraphrase from an article by Bill Fink: "A tackle dealer named Hiram Brobst encountered the pattern in an eighteenth century English angling book. The fly was not identified, so Hiram called it the 'No Name.' The pattern became known throughout Pennsylvania in the '20's and '30's. Because of its extreme popularity in the Henryville area of the Poconos, the fly was rechristened the 'Henryville.' "

Henryville

Hook:	Mustad-Viking 94840 (regular dry fly); 14 - 22
Thread:	black 6/0 nylon
Body:	green floss
Palmer Body Hackle:	grizzly rooster hackle (trimmed on top)
Under Wing:	wood duck fibers (sparse)
Over Wing:	matched slips of slate duck quill (flat over back)
Head Hackle:	dark ginger rooster hackle

Buttonwood

This fly is a companion pattern of the Henryville; similarly named after a famous pool on the private water of the Paradise Branch of the Brodhead River.

Hook:	Mustad-Viking 94840; 18 - 22
Body:	white floss
Thread:	white 6/0 nylon
Palmer Body Hackle:	grizzly rooster hackle (trimmed on top)
Wing:	matched slips of slate duck quill (flat over back)
Head Hackle:	light ginger rooster hackle

NYMPH PATTERNS

WEIGHTED NYMPHS

On Colorado streams, the art of the deep nymph is a cult akin to a religion. Anglers of the region are masters of the technique. As more of these fly fishermen relocate to other trout-areas of the country, they form a spreading web of disciples who demonstrate the effectiveness of the deep nymph on rivers and streams everywhere.

Chuck Fothergill, the eloquent priest of the weighted-presentation, carries the gospel both through personal teaching and writing — excerpts of a letter to the author include comments on the historical development of the technique in the Aspen area:

> I first came into contact with the weighted fly/leader approach while fishing primarily on the South Platte River when I lived in Denver. The proponent of the method then — the man from whom I learned — was Ralph Smith. He's still a proponent — and a good one!
>
> When I arrived here in Aspen, no one even knew what a nymph was. Through my promoting, teaching, and demonstrating the effectiveness of the deep nymph technique, the use now is as commonplace here as eating lunch at noontime. This turnaround by the local anglers started in 1965 — the first summer I lived here. Everyone then fished either dry or downstream wet. The upstream nymph was something completely new. Other anglers would fish a day and take 10 or 12 fish and on the same day I'd take 40 or 50, and thereby the method began to get their attention as well as their questions.
>
> It is very difficult for a serious fly fisherman to avoid some sort of nymph indoctrination if he lives close to Aspen. As to 'experts' whom

198

I've seen become very proficient with the method, there are several here in the area —

Charlie Loughridge   George Odier

Terry Ross   Bob Simons

The above are but a few, but they really know their stuff when it comes to fishing the nymph. They also act as guides out of my store, so they have the ability of teaching nymph fishing as well as practising it.

Whenever and wherever I fish, I use nymphs the majority of the time. The greatest percentage of a trout's feeding is done near the bottom of our rivers, and it just follows that the proper pattern and presentation will take fish — whether in New York, Michigan, Montana, Oregon, or Colorado. To be general — I feel that this angling method should be effective on almost all trout rivers.

Bel Berean owns the Western Angler fly shop in Missoula. As a transplant from Colorado to Montana, he is familiar with the entire region. He recommends the following basic selection of weighted nymphs (smaller sizes for winter use):

Gray Nymph

      Hook: Mustad-Viking 7957 (long shank; extra strong); 10 - 18

      Tail: fibers of badger hair (sparse)

      Body: muskrat fur (dubbed rough with guard hairs)

      Hackle: grizzly hen hackle (several turns as a collar)

Zug Bug

      Hook: Mustad-Viking 9671 (2X long); 8 - 18

      Tail: peacock sword herl (3 strands)

      Body: peacock herl (thicker wrap at thorax)

      Wing Cases: mallard flank feather (covert)

      Hackle: brown hen hackle

Brassy

> *Hook:* Mustad-Viking 94840 (extra fine wire); 16 - 20
> *Tail:* brown hen hackle fibers (sparse)
> *Body:* fine brass wire (tapered over a base of wool)
> *Hackle:* brown hen hackle (tied down in a beard hackle)

Montana Nymph

> *Hook:* Mustad-Viking 9672 (3X long); 6 - 12
> *Tail:* matched slips of black crow feather
> *Abdomen:* black chenille
> *Thorax:* yellow chenille
> *Wing Pad:* 2 strands of black chenille (tied down over the thorax and hackle)
> *Hackle:* black cock hackle (palmered over the thorax)

Gold Ribbed Hare's Ear

> *Hook:* Mustad-Viking 7957; 8 - 18
> *Tail:* brown hen hackle fibers
> *Abdomen:* speckled fur from a European hare's ear
> *Ribbing:* oval gold tinsel (over the abdomen)
> *Thorax:* fur from a hare's ear (dubbed rough — guard hairs picked out to represent legs)
> *Wing Pad:* grey duck quill section (covert)

Trueblood's Otter Nymph

> *Hook:* Mustad-Viking 7957; 12 - 18
> *Tail:* speckled partridge fibers
> *Body:* dubbing of otter fur (a lighter shade of dubbing from the belly section)
> *Hackle:* speckled partridge wisps (beard)

Blackfly Larva

Hook:	Mustad-Viking 7948 A (regular); 16 - 20
Thread:	black 6/0 nylon
Body:	dark blackish olive rayon floss
Thorax:	dark blackish olive rayon floss
Ribbing:	fine silver wire

(The body/thorax is formed in the shape of a taper such as a bowling pin.)

This pattern is listed in *Nymphs* — the Ernest Schwiebert angling/entomology classic, which comprehensively relates the important lesser forms of aquatic insects.

The following technique is effective for stream trout: the final section of a standard leader is replaced with a tippet of white sewing thread or white horse hair. A small dark wet fly is played downstream, a free drift interspersed with slight tugs of the line.

This was a method used by old-time anglers, who clipped the wings of a Black Gnat down to stubs. In June and July, the trick of the white thread fooled brook trout in Maine. On the riffles of small streams, the small Gnat accounted for the 50 to 100-fish baskets.

The white thread simulates the "anchor line" of the larva of the blackfly *(Simulium)*. The larva clings to rocks in aerated water with the posterior sucker attached to a stone surface. If the insect is·dislodged or swept from its hold by the current, a white silken excretion unfurls from the contact point. The larva, dangling in the flow, draws the line to regain the safety of the stone.

Dense colonies of blackfly crust the stones of high-nutrient waters in a living mass: the infamous biting species *(S. hirtipes)* in the East and the abundant Buffalo Gnat species *(S. tuberosum)* in the West. The distinctive action of disoriented larva serves as the trigger characteristic. The thread exposes a vulnerability that excites the interest and the strike of a trout.

201

Natural Drift
Stone Fly Nymph *(Pteronarcys — salmon fly)*

Under the surface, a river is a jumble of images, each image lasting only a moment. Drift objects scuttle on a weave of currents. Sunlit refracts with the uneven shimmer of the meniscus, and colors soften to the muted tones of a water-paint wash.

For trout, the most distinguishing characteristic of an underwater organism is its motion-index. Trout establish a rhythm of selective feeding keyed to motion index.

Shape, size, and color are less important than movement as the imitative factor for an artificial fly — only the luminescent quality of a pattern is as critical, in certain instances, as the technique of presentation.

The construction of a fly affects its realistic action. The pattern behaves with a specific sink-rate, position balance, or swim-action in accordance with the physical bulk and displacement weight of its materials. A correctly tied fly responds to water forces or to manipulations of the angler in simulating the natural action of a prey organism.

> *Hook:* Mustad-Viking 9671 (2X long); 4, 6, 8
> Thread: black 2/0 nylon
> *Tail:* pheasant tail feather fibers (2 - tied split)
> *Abdomen:* dubbed brown fur
> *Ribbing:* stripped quill of a brown cock feather
> *Thorax:* spun black deer body hair (clipped to
> front-tapered shape)
> *Hackle:* furnace rooster hackle (palmered snugly
> into the thorax hair)

(Before tying, the hook is bent into a 45 degree angle at the planned juncture of thorax and abdomen. The abdomen alone is weighted with lead wire strips, under-fastened on each side of the shank.)

As the natural *Pteronarcys* nymph is jostled or swept off its hold on the bottom rocks, the insect lapses into an inert state of shock. As it drifts with the current, the nymph curls the thorax forward. The body position bal-

202

ances as the insect washes along in partially upright stability, until at a downstream stretch of suitable riffle the nymph wiggles in a clumsy swim towards the bottom sanctuary.

The Natural-drift Stonefly simulates the behavior of the actual nymph. With a wrap of lead wire weight 18 inches up the leader, the pattern drifts at the up-cant. Tugs of current manipulate the fly to represent the insect's beginning struggle to swim to the bottom strata.

F. B. POTTS' MITE PATTERNS

No set of flies is more exclusively typical of Montana than the Mite series, the patterns that feature a woven hackle of stiff hair. The collar of fibers is distinctly suited to swift rivers of mountain regions. The hair withstands the press of the strongest flow, retaining its life-like identity in the current.

The theory of matching the physical resilience of materials to the water is not a new idea. H. C. Cutcliffe, in the early 1800's in *Trout Fishing in Rapid Streams,* noted, "All hackles should be plucked from a cock's neck; hen hackles are worse than useless in rapid streams; they have no stiffness, cannot resist the force of water washing on them and consequently lie flat along the hook."

George F. Grant, an acknowledged authority on the woven hair hackle in his own *The Art of Weaving Hair Hackles,* comments on the observations of H. C. Cutcliffe and Roger Wooley, "When it is considered that these eminent English authorities were concerned with the fast, rocky streams of Yorkshire and Devonshire, mere brooks in comparison with the Madison River, it is obvious that flies made with feather hackles are unsuitable for our western rivers."

Frank B. Potts originated the concept of the hair hackle for the artificial fly. The wig-maker utilized techniques of weaving in using bristling fibers of ox hair. Commercial production of his patented patterns started in the 1930's in a small upstairs loft in Missoula.

The Mite flies are still distributed throughout western Montana by Gene Snyder of the Angler's Roost in Hamilton, and over 30 patterns of the series are available at local tackle shops. Among resident fly fishermen, the Sandy Mite-Lady Mite-Mr. Mite set are still the most popular wet patterns for swift streams of the region.

Sandy Mite

Hook:	Mustad-Viking 7958 (reversed)
Body:	light sandy ox hair
Woven Stripe:	orange thread
Hackle:	light sandy ox hair

Lady Mite

Hook:	Mustad-Viking 7958 (reversed)
Body:	badger hair (the dark section of the hair is wound in 3 turns at the bend of the hook)
Woven Stripe:	orange thread
Hackle:	badger hair

Mr. Mite

Hook:	Mustad-Viking 7958 (reversed)
Body:	dark chocolate brown ox hair
Woven Stripe:	orange thread
Hackle:	dark chocolate brown ox hair

204

This series of Mite flies is not nationally prominent. Outside of western Montana/northern Idaho, the patterns are not known, but there is no reason why the Mite concept might not prove valuable for fast-water rivers elsewhere in the country.

The unique techniques for tying the woven hackle and the woven body for Mite patterns are thoroughly explained in *The Art of Weaving the Hair Hackles* and *Montana Trout Flies,* by George F. Grant.

WET FLY PATTERNS

STANDARD WET FLY FAVORITES

"The classic wet fly approach is an outdated method, the technique preempted by the development of subsurface nymph and bucktail imitations" — such is the litany offered in the modern code of fly fishing. But in truth, neither the nymph nor the bucktail replaces effective use of the wet fly, and for this reason revival of standard patterns again finds a niche in the repertoire of a versatile fly fisherman.

205

Alexandria

This fly was a primary culprit-pattern responsible for so decimating the trout population of the Itchen that the standard wet fly was banned from the private water of this chalk stream.

Hook:	Mustad-Viking 7957-B (long shank)
Tip:	dark red floss
Tail:	8 or 9 strands of peacock sword
Body:	flat silver tinsel
Ribbing:	oval silver tinsel
Wing:	peacock sword 15 to 20 strands
Hackle:	black hen hackle

Perkin's Pet

This simple bedraggled fly is a contender for the title of most undistinguished pattern. A small Perkin's Pet is a searching fly for gentle drifts in holding spots of a stream.

Hook:	Mustad-Viking 7957-B
Body:	silver floss (substituted for silver tinsel)
Hackle:	brown palmer rooster hackle (short)
Wing:	slate grey duck quill

Yellow Coachman

For rainbow trout, I prefer the yellow center joint rather than the red floss of the Royal Coachman. With a darting swim, this pattern is deadly in a deep swing close to the bottom.

Hook:	Mustad-Viking 7957-B
Tail:	coachman brown hackle fibers
Aft Butt:	peacock herl strands
Center Joint:	yellow floss
Fore Butt:	peacock herl strands
Wing:	white duck quill
Hackle:	coachman brown hen hackle (sparse collar)

Orange Fish Hawk

A venerable angling axiom opts for a bright fly on a bright day. In practice, this pattern is very effective on sunshine days.

> *Hook:* Mustad-Viking 7957-B
> *Body:* orange floss
> *Ribbing:* fine gold tinsel
> *Hackle:* light badger rooster hackle
> (a collar hackle tied to slant back)

Hare's Ear

The mottled mix of Hare's Ear fur is a naturally impressionistic dubbing. As a realistic imitation, this famed pattern is effective with a feeble stutter drift.

> *Hook:* Mustad-Viking 7957-B
> *Body:* Hare's Ear fur (roughly dubbed)
> *Wing:* grey slate duck quill
> *Hackle:* guard hairs of the fur — picked out

Montreal

This pattern is a brook trout standard that is surprisingly deadly on brown trout in the early hours after dawn.

> *Hook:* Mustad-Viking 7957-B
> *Tip:* narrow gold tinsel
> *Tail:* scarlet hen hackle fibers
> *Body:* claret floss
> *Ribbing:* narrow gold tinsel
> *Wing:* brown turkey quill
> *Hackle:* claret hen hackle

207

Rube Wood

This white grub pattern with a puffed body of chenille is a mystery — a fly that bedevils fussy trout, although it is too bright to resemble basic insect fare.

> *Hook:* Mustad-Viking 7957-B
> *Tail:* teal fibers (sparse)
> *Tip:* scarlet floss
> *Body:* white chenille
> *Wing:* grey mallard fibers (flat over back)
> *Hackle:* brown hen hackle (very sparse collar)

Light Hendrickson

The Hendrickson as a dry fly or a wet fly is an excellent imitation in small sizes (16 - 18 - 20) for pale-shade mayflies. During an insect emergence, the wet pattern often fools trout that feed selectively on top fare, the same fish accepting the general imitation of the wet fly.

> *Hook:* Mustad-Viking 7957-B
> *Tail:* woodduck fibers
> *Body:* light fox belly fur
> *Wing:* wood duck fibers
> *Hackle:* pale blue dun hen hackle

The Gimp — A fine wet fly, originated by Lacy Gee; listed in the paper-
back booklet *Practical Flies and Their Construction.*

    The Gimp is a natural-life fly, which by either sight-appearance or
natural action inherent in the materials, tempts trout from routine fare to
sample an available delicacy. It is characteristic of especially effective
sub-surface flies: imitative qualities are achieved through construction of
the fly.

    Natural-effect patterns are not the only flies which catch fish — or not
even the flies which catch most fish. In the hands of a skilled fisherman,
any accumulation of fur or feather or tinsel will fool trout, but the art of
catching trout is then more dependent on the manipulative intrigue of the
angler. The trend of fly fishing now is towards an imitative ideal of
impressionistic simulation; although angling on the basis of a theory of
attraction demands greater skill for consistent success, the classic wet fly
approach is rarely employed now on trout streams.

    The wet fly or bucktail angler searches for a precise life-effect of his
imitation. The naturalness of the fly is predicated on three factors —
currents, pattern materials, and induced actions. The fisherman controls
the motion of the fly: the more action imparted by the flow or inherent in
the pattern, the more subtle the play of the cast.

    The Gimp is a creation fished singly on a fine tippet in a slow water
habitat. The soft materials wash enticingly with each twitch of the rod tip,
the pattern working with a gentle tease approach neither too erratically
nor too quickly. The undulant allure of the fly lends realism even in slow
motion.

Hook:	Mustad-Sproat 3906
Thread:	black 6/0 nylon
Tail:	dark blue dun hen hackle fibers
Body:	grey wool (wrapped almost plump)
Wing:	soft dun under-feathers beneath the
	tippets of an Amherst pheasant neck
	(two tied flat on top of the hook shank)
Hackle:	dark blue dun hen hackle
	(two turns of a collar wrap)

The Black June — A hair wing adaption

Hook:	Mustad-Sproat 3906
Tag:	fine flat silver tinsel
Body:	peacock herl
Ribbing:	embossed silver tinsel (only 3 turns)
Wing:	black hair of the Monga Ring-Tail
Hackle:	black hen hackle (wrapped as a
	sparse collar)

(standard version listed in *Trout,*
by Ray Bergman)

    Inspiration for a pattern often lies in the clutter scattered over the table of a flytier. In the process of fly tying, there are waste materials, but often discarded fragments from popular standards are the ingredients of merit for effective new creations.

    In the course of tying 40 or 50 dozen Royal Trude dry flies with the fine white hair of the Monga Ring-Tail, I was left with bands of interspersed black hair remaining on each skin. I picked a standard wet fly with a black wing for tying in the common hair-wing adaption, and after an evening's work ended up with a supply of Black June flies.

    I stashed a few of this pattern type in the corner of a wet fly book, but most of the flies were sent as trades to angling friends. I thought no more of the obscure little fly through the early part of the season, but during the summer, I received a letter from the fine fly fisherwoman, L. O. "Sandy"

Sage, "...a great little beetle imitation. The trout were stuffed with beetles."

The Black June, with a flat carapace of hair over the body of irridescent herl and reflective tinsel, proved to be a fine imitation of an aquatic diving beetle. Among weedy channels of spring-creeks, which harbored an abundance of beetles *(Coleoptera),* the wet fly fooled choosy trout.

Among an angler's pattern stock, there is a consistent need for a predominantly black wet fly. In weak light on a stream or pond, a dark pattern casts a sharp silhouette against a mottled background. The Black June with its realistic shape of a common aquatic insect effectively substitutes for the Black Gnat or the Black Angel as an all-around black teaser.

MINNOW-FLY PATTERNS

A minnow imitation is less popular than other fly types on trout streams, and not surprisingly it is the least understood of fly fishing tools. Too often the bucktail is relegated to special circumstances — high spring-time flows or big rivers or trophy fish habitats; but actually the minnow fly is a pattern for all seasons. A subtle imitative style is valuable in high-visibility water; a flashy attractor style is indispensable in low-visibility water. Fishing the bucktail/streamer is a technique for arousing the fine fish that persist even in heavy-pressure streams and ponds.

STREAMERS

Golden Witch

This Carrie Stevens pattern of barred silver and gold tints imitates open-water bait fish (barred killifish, for example). At the dawn or dusk time of minnow chasers, the fly yields fine results with a moderate strip retrieve across the shallows.

Hook:	Mustad-Viking 9674 (4X long); 8, 10
Thread:	black 4/0 nylon (a band of red thread centered on the head)
Tag:	narrow flat silver tinsel
Body:	orange floss (thin)
Ribbing:	narrow flat silver tinsel
Underwing:	4 strands of peacock herl
Overwing:	4 grizzly saddle hackles
Throat:	white bucktail (sparse) to the barb of the hook — grizzly hackle fibers beneath the hair (short)
Shoulders:	golden pheasant tippets (1 on each side — ⅓ as long as the hackles)
Cheeks:	imitation jungle cock (short)

Gray Ghost

This imitation of the smelt of Maine lakes is the most famous Carrie Stevens creation. The pattern is a proven favorite for ouananiche and squaretails of the Northland, but similarly it is a killing fly in most rivers and lakes across the country. The Ghost produces with its slim-line form even in those waters that contain no bait fish resembling the prototype smelt.

212

Hook:	Mustad-Viking 9674 (4X long); 4, 6, 8
Thread:	black 4/0 nylon (a band of red thread centered on the head)
Tag:	flat silver tinsel (narrow)
Body:	orange floss (thin)
Ribbing:	flat silver tinsel (narrow)
Throat:	four or five strands of peacock herl beyond the barb of the hook); a sparse bunch of white bucktail (beyond the barb of the hook); a golden pheasant crest feather (as long as the shoulder — curving upward)
Underwing:	a golden pheasant crest feather (curving downward)
Overwing:	four olive-grey saddle hackles
Shoulders:	a Ripon's silver pheasant body feather (on each side — ⅓ as long as the wing)
Cheeks:	imitation jungle cock

Lord Iris

Preston Jennings was always an inquisitive angler and scientific innovator, who patterned the Lord Iris to match a prismatic breakdown of the colors of the common minnow. A play of shading in the fly simulates the varying color-picture of the active bait fish.

This concept of imitation was intriguing enough to investigate by scuba observation; indeed, the fly in the water acquired an impressionistic reality. With a constant-motion retrieve, the small sizes of the bright pattern performed well during a day for the unpredictable fish of the Boulder River.

Hook:	Mustad-Viking 9672 (3X long); 10, 12, 14
Thread:	black 6/0 nylon
Tail:	matched sections of married red, blue, and yellow goose feather (narrow — in order from top to bottom)

213

Body:	medium flat silver tinsel
Ribbing:	narrow oval silver tinsel
Wing:	4 ginger furnace hackles
Shoulders:	narrow matched sections of red, blue, and yellow goose feather — ⅔ as long as the wing (laying along the top of the wing)
Cheeks:	imitation jungle cock
Throat:	yellow saddle hackle (beard)

Black and White (Austin Hogan)

With the coming of night, the sensitive cone cells of a fish's eye recede until color is no longer distinguishable. In the dim evening, it is the contrast of the pattern, not the color, that is important for visual recognition.

The feather wing of the Black and White achieves contrast with a unique blending technique. The bottom halves of the outside black hackles of the wing are stripped away to expose the inside white hackles, lending an aesthetic appeal to the common black and white color-scheme.

Hook:	Mustad-Viking 79580 (4X long); 6, 8
Thread:	black 4/0 nylon
Tail:	crimson hackle fibers (small bunch)
Body:	narrow flat silver tinsel
Throat:	10 or 12 pink bucktail hairs (longer than the hook); mixed with a sparse bunch of crimson hackle fibers (half the length of the hair)
Inside Wing:	4 white saddle hackles
Outside Wing:	2 black saddle hackles (one on each side — the fibers on the bottom of the black feathers stripped off)
Shoulders:	black mallard body feather (⅓ as long as the wing)
Cheeks:	imitation jungle cock

214

Light Spruce (originally patterned for sea-run cutthroat on coastal rivers
— credited to a man named Godfrey)

This splay-wing pattern is one of the few feather streamers to gain extensive acceptance in the West. Throughout the mountain region, the fly holds a reputation as a large trout deceiver. On the broad expanses of big rivers — Yellowstone, Snake, Green — the action-attractor consistently busts fish from glory holes.

Hook:	Mustad-Limerick 3123 (regular shank length); 1, 2, 4
Thread:	black 4/0 nylon
Tail:	4 or 5 peacock sword fibers (short)
Body:	scarlet floss
Forward Butt:	peacock herl (dressed heavy)
Wing:	2 silver badger rooster hackles (tied back to back to curve outward — slightly longer than the tail)
Hackle:	silver badger rooster hackle (a bushy collar hackle slanted back around the fly)

BUCKTAILS

Miller's River Special (Paul Kukonen and Henry Scarborough)

Local custom deserves just due, so before a day of casting the Miller's River, I tied a few of the namesake pattern. The fly indeed performed in a special manner on this river in Massachusetts, and it also succeeded on other occasions on streams all over the country.

Hook:	Mustad-Viking 79580 (4X long); 8, 10, 12
Tail:	golden pheasant tipped fibers (extended slightly beyond the hook bend)
Body:	flat gold tinsel

Ribbing: oval gold tinsel
Wing: yellow bucktail (small bunch);
black bucktail (small bunch — on top);
extending beyond the end of the tail
Shoulders: golden pheasant red side feather (half
as long as the wing — tied horizontally)
Cheeks: imitation jungle cock (short)

Little Rainbow Trout (Samuel R. Slaymaker II)

Wherever rainbow trout exist in a natural population, this fly acts as a taunt to large fish both as a food item and as a territorial threat, when it is teased through solitary lairs.

Hook: Mustad-Limerick 3665-A (½ inch longer
than regular shank); 4, 6, 8, 10
Thread: black 4/0 nylon
Tail: bright green bucktail (small bunch)
Body: pinkish white spun fur
Ribbing: narrow flat silver tinsel
Throat: pink bucktail (extending to the tail)
Wing: 4 sparse bunches of hair (each
extending slightly beyond the tail)
— white bucktail; pink bucktail; bright
breen bucktail; natural badger hair
(applied in order from bottom to top)
Cheeks: imitation jungle cock

Mickey Finn

There is an intrinsic mystery about an attractor pattern. An angler cannot know future results — an inspired success or a momentous dud. One day — bam; the next day — flat; all on the same water.

Hook: Mustad-Viking 79580 (4X long);
8, 10, 12, 14
Thread: black 4/0 nylon
Body: flat silver tinsel
Ribbing: oval silver tinsel
Wing: 3 slim bunches of bucktail — yellow
bucktail; red bucktail; yellow bucktail
(twice as wide as lower two bunches)

Dark Edson Tiger (William Edson)

This pattern relies upon universal colors — yellow and speckled brown — that predominate in the underwater view. As a general realistic imitation, the natural appearance of the fly is perfect.

Hook: Mustad-Viking 79580 (4X long);
6, 8, 10
Thread: black 4/0 nylon
Tag: narrow flat gold tinsel
Tail: barred wood duck (two bars visible)
Body: peacock herl
Wing: yellow bucktail (shy of the bend of
the hook)
Shoulders: red rooster hackles (along the top of the wing)
Cheeks: imitation jungle cock (short)

Black Nosed Dace (Art Flick)

The concept of matching a minnow is as valid as the practice of imitating an insect. A fly cast to simulate the actions of a prevalent bait fish fools warier trout. This pattern manipulated to mimic the dart of a small dace turns respectable hold-over fish of Eastern streams.

217

Hook:	Mustad-Viking 79580 (4X long);
	4, 6, 8, 10
Thread:	black 4/0 nylon
Tail:	red yarn (short)
Body:	flat silver tinsel
Ribbing:	oval silver tinsel
Wing:	sparse bunches of bucktail — white
	bucktail; black bucktail; brown bucktail
	(applied in order from bottom to top)

The Hornberg — A favorite (originated by Frank Hornberg)

Hook:	Mustad-Viking 7948-A (regular);
	4, 6, 8, 10
Body:	flat silver tinsel
Inside Wing:	two yellow rooster hackles (barely visible)
Outside Wing:	barred mallard breast feathers
Cheeks:	jungle cock imitation (long)
Hackle:	light badger rooster hackle (bushy
	collar dry fly style)

This pattern is a versatile creation. Fished dry or wet in any direction, it simulates a vibrancy of life. No matter what motion is imparted, the fly responds with a balanced swim. From any view, the Hornberg always looks right in the water. The same quotation that explains the universal effectiveness of the Muddler Minnow applies to the Hornberg: "There is no way to fish it wrong."

Muddler Minnow (originated by Don Gapen)

Hook:	Mustad-Viking 9672 (3X long); 1, 2, 4, 6, 8, 10
Thread:	grey 2/0 nylon
Head:	natural grey deer body hair
Tail:	matched slips of brown mottled turkey quill
Body:	flat gold tinsel
Feather Wing:	matched sections of brown mottled turkey quill
Hair Wing:	fox squirrel tail hair

The bulk of the head, shaping a blunt front on the Muddler Minnow, was not a unique innovation, but an effect achieved with mid-1800 salmon flies by a wrap of herl; but a shag of deer hair with a collar flare significantly altered the bucktail composition in both appearance and swim-action. The silhouette successfully portrayed the thickened shoulders of the sculpin, and the life-shimmer imitated the uncertain swimming ability of the prey-fish.

Dan Gapen sketched the history of the commercial boom of the pattern in a letter to the author:

> The Muddler was designed for use on a fly rod. The first size ever made was a No. 4, which matched the natural cockatush minnow well. Big brook trout (speckles — square tails) were the target. The fly was originated in the summer of 1937 by my father.
>
> The fly was fished in the rapid water of the old Nipigon River, in most cases in the quiet pools. Here the fly was wetted by mouth with saliva, to make the deer hair sink better, and fished across current in a slow retrieve.
>
> The name of the fly is derived from the sculpin minnow, which is called the Muddler in southern Wisconsin where my grandfather

originated. All three minnows are of the sculpin family, whether called Sculpin, Muddler, or Cockatush. Cockatush is the Ojibiwa name for the sculpin in northern Ontario.

The fly first became of real commercial value after Al McClane and Joe Brooks wrote articles in *Field & Stream* and *Outdoor Life* in the early '40's. We, of course, were tying them for distribution in the Canadian market prior to this, but the increase in sales really started right after World War II. We sold our first ones commercially in the summer of 1939 to tourists at the resort.

At present, the Muddler still remains our top selling single fly. Over 18,000 dozen are sold each year. As the public discovers the disadvantages of the foreign-made imitations, this volume seems to increase. We are presently shipping this fly to eleven foreign countries simply because they want the original.

I've personally fished the fly from the southern reaches of South America to the Arctic, taking most species of gamefish in salt water or fresh water. Though I have access to over 300 varieties of fly, about 85% of my fly fishing is done with the Muddlers in various sizes.

The riddle of near-universal effectiveness of the Muddler for all species of trout in all types of habitat is partially explained by an appearance that parallels the typical color drabness of underwater life. The fly is not solely an imitation of the *Cottus* sculpin. Manipulated to simulate the motion habit of a specific prey organism, the pattern also represents mad-tom and stoneroller minnows, grasshoppers, and nymphs of the *Pteronarcys* stone fly; and it imitates the general form of other delicacies, including moths, dragonfly larvae, and crawfish.

Joe Brooks tabbed the Muddler Minnow the most potent trout fly, noting in the *Complete Book of Fly Fishing,* "How one bucktail can look like so many different things is a great puzzle, but whatever it happens to look like at the moment, it always seems to look good to the trout."

As the fame of the Muddler spread after initial publicity, the pattern was adopted by commercial tiers everywhere. Inevitably the fly was tied in alternate styles. The original Muddler was constructed with a shaggy and sparse head in a pattern that swam below surface with a vibrant undulation to represent movements of the natural minnow; but two early deviations of head style were tied with densely spun and evenly clipped deer hair, either in a concave-face shape or a tapering-bullet shape. The

220

alternate patterns were more buoyant flies with a different swim-action; they were effective imitations for certain natural items but not as effective as the shaggy original for minnow imitation.

Many fine fly fishermen who fish the fly and qualify as Muddler experts, sent samples of their preferred tie. The flies were stored in a non-use felt book, each leaf labelled by name: Art Aylesworth, Walt Burr, J. Marshal Edmonds, Graydon Fenn, Joe Garman, Ed LaGava, Joe Maley. Although these anglers lived and fished in different trout-sections of the country, the linking characteristic of the sample flies was the same shaggy roughness dressed into the original Muddler.

In college, tying patterns commercially, I prepared 10 dozen Muddlers. I carefully clipped neat heads, seated straight wings, and lacquered smooth bodies, dressing the flies as much for praise from a master fly fisherman as for income.

I handed a plastic bag with the Muddler flies to Dick Fryhover, before we started a day of angling. He took one fly out and held it up. "Perfect," he said, carefully putting the No. 10 pattern back into the sack.

As we arrived at the lake, he again pulled out a Muddler. "You know, you don't tie flies — you create them."

While he was talking, his fingers were splitting strands of wing fibers, pinching bits of hollow deer hair, snapping tufts of squirrel hair. He completed the task of desecration by dropping the fly to the dirt and grinding it with the toe of his boot. He primped the frayed remnant. "And now," he squinted, "it's ready to catch fish."

It took a long time before I understood his preference for the unsaleable fly for actual fishing. Just as I learned so many other facets of fly fishing from Dick, he revealed the secret of the shaggy pattern: at moments, ugly is exquisite to trout.

TYING INSTRUCTIONS FOR THE HAIR-SPUN PATTERN

These construction tips for the durable spun-hair fly are possibly too time consuming for the commercial producer, but the hints are valuable for the discriminating amateur tier.

221

Hook: Mustad-Viking 9672

Thread: grey 2/0 nylon

(the author does not recommend
Nymo nylon — it eventually stretches
to loosen the bind on the deer hair)

Tail: mottled brown turkey quill

1. Match the slips of oak turkey from a pair of opposite quill feathers.

2. Grasp the slips firmly in the thumb and the index finger of the left hand — dull side to dull side.

3. Hold the bottom edge of the butts of the feathers upright over the top of the hook shank at the bend.

4. Drop a loose loop of thread over the shank — the thread held over the butts in the same pinch of the thumb and the finger.

5. Pull the thread down with a snap to seat the slips straight on top of the shank.

Body: flat gold tinsel

1. Wind the thread ⅔ up the hook shank.

2. Tie in the tinsel with the tag end pointing to the rear.

3. Snip the excess of the stub closely at a slant.

4. Wind the tinsel in even wraps back to the bend — return the wrap to the front to the spot ahead of the tie-in point.

5. Tie down — coat the tinsel with clear lacquer to retard tarnish.

Hair Wing: fox squirrel tail hair

> 1. Fasten on top of the shank 15 or 20 hairs of fox squirrel tail (extended to the bend of the hook).
>
> 2. Clip the butts of the hair at a forward diagonal.
>
> 3. Cement the stubs.

Feather Wing: mottled brown turkey quill

(the preference is for wide slats)

> Repeat the procedure for the tail slips. Half-hitch the tie-down.

Head: natural grey deer body hair

> (Select the length of hair on the deer skin for the size of the fly — the shorter natural hair for the smaller pattern size.)
>
> 1. Position the thread between the hook eye and the wrap-off of the turkey wing.
>
> 2. Cement the area behind the hook eye.

Preparation of the deer hair –

> Clip the hair from the skin at the base of the fibers. Hold the hair tips in the left hand, stroking the bunch with the fingers of the right hand to shake loose the short ill-formed bits of hair. Pluck free the fine fuzz at the base of the clump of hair.
>
> Apply the hair in two or three bunches — allowing better binding.
>
> 1. Lay a bunch of hair with the tips extending back along the hook shank.

2. Wrap the thread firmly over the hair (a fastening loop).

3. Pull the thread tight to flare the hair — with the finger tips, further primp the hair to stand straight.

4. Wind binding loops of the thread with a slight side to side sawing motion to work it deep to the base.

5. Wind the thread with an X-pattern — first through the standing hair to the back and second through the standing hair to the front (better than wrapping in a continuous line over the same spot).

Apply hair in additional bunches in the same manner to evenly encircle the shank (the type of head the tyer wants is determined by the density of hair laid around the shank — sparse for a shag head or thick for a concave head).

1. Whip finish.

2. Clip the head to the desired form (leaving a flair of hair tips extending back around the hook shank).

Common variations in the standard dressing of the Muddler Minnow:

1. Gold tinsel is replaced with a white or cream shade of wool for the body (especially in the smooth flow of clear water the bright flash of metal detracts from a realistic imitation of a drab-colored minnow).

2. To produce a more mottled brown tone in the pattern, the fox squirrel tail hair is replaced with red squirrel hair.

3. Grey turkey feather is used for the tail
and wing to add a grey cast.

SELECTING THE HEAD-TYPE OF THE SPUN HAIR FLY

As he carried samples of the Muddler Minnow to trout spots around the world, Joe Brooks served as ambassador for the pattern. He took the fly to Montana, where he tested it successfully on browns and rainbows of the Yellowstone River. One of the people to whom he showed the fly was Dan Bailey of Livingston.

Possibly to better simulate the shoulder thickness of the natural sculpin, Dan Bailey altered the head-style of the Muddler to a dense-spun concave shape. This form of the fly more exactly imitated the minnow, but the high buoyancy of the pattern failed to simulate the bottom-hugging habit of the sculpin; and yet the redesigned Muddler caught trout in great numbers. Along grasshopper-rich Western rivers, the Muddler broke out lunker fish. The new Muddler blossomed as a big trout lure as innovative anglers developed techniques to fit the concave style. The fly, fished subtly as a grasshopper pattern, established the Montana region as the seat of Muddler reputation.

Other commercial tiers incorporated the dense-spun bullet shape, producing a slimmer pattern effective with both a shallow darting retrieve and a dead drift. Less buoyant with more of the hair clipped, this shape allowed a realistic drift with the head riding vertically in the water in the wash-manner of common stone fly nymphs.

A relatively recent variation of clip-style emerged as an off-shoot pattern of the Muddler: a flat V trimmed on the bottom, with a taper to a triangular crest at the top. This shape retained width of head without increasing undue bouyancy of spun-hair. For the weighted fly, the new head style abetted a more rapid sink-rate.

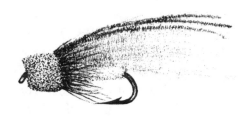

Standard Marabou Muddler — adapted by Dan Bailey

The Muddler Minnow style was so distinctive that inevitably there were variations on the common theme. These new patterns used the unifying characteristic of the spun-hair head. None of the altered versions replaced the Muddler as a supreme general-use fly, but variations in color or materials pinpointed the value of different types for specific moments.

An early variety combined the hair flare with the intrinsic lure of marabou feathers. The fly was tied with a body of tinsel chenille that added to its attraction. This pattern gained its fame on Western rivers by tallying impressive totals of lunker trout, many of which are traced in outline on the Wall of Fame at Dan Bailey's Fly Shop.

Hook: Mustad-Viking 9672; 6, 4, 2
Thread: grey 2/0 nylon
Body: gold tinsel chenille
Wing: marabou feather stalks (tips of two feathers)
Head: natural grey deer body hair (concave style)

(Wet the marabou feathers before tying to
better judge the length to the bend of the hook.)

The buoyancy of fluffy marabou feathers plus a dense clip of hollow spun-hair limits the unweighted fly to near-surface fishing. The soft marabou breathes in quiet-water edges and pools of a stream. Tugged against the current, the wing waves in the flow of the water.

At night, a white or a black Marabou Muddler attracts by sound as well as by sight-silhouette. A greased fly burbles when a twitch scoops the concave face against the surface. The pattern is played slowly or steadily rather than too erratically, with a swimming movement that presents an easy target for a charging fish.

Plain Jane

Hook: Mustad-Viking 9672; 10, 12
Thread: grey 2/0 nylon
Wing: marabou fibers (sparse application —
extending only as long as
the bend of the hook)
Body: eggshell white wool yarn
Tail: marabou fibers (thick bunch — a short
¼ inch extension beyond the bend)
Head: natural grey deer body hair
(clipped shaggy)

Favorite colors (wing and tail matching) —
brown, grey, dark green, or black

The standard Marabou Muddler, with a tinsel chenille body and a flare of marabou, is an attractor fly. It excites trout to a frenzy; often fish

227

nip, jump, or tail-slap the fly. But at times, with clear-water conditions, trout ignore the pattern.

The Plain Jane is a more subtle variation. In its simplicity of form, it poses as both an attractor and an imitator. The fly elicits an attack, but it draws fish from beyond predator distance, catching finicky trout that spurn a brighter fly.

GENERAL VARIATIONS OF THE MUDDLER MINNOW

Mizzoolian Spook — originated by Vince Hamlin
(creator of the *Alley Oop* comic strip)

Each trout season, in the early days of September, there is a flux of water on the Clark Fork near Deer Lodge, as the irrigation ponds are released at the end of the pumping season. The flow is tainted for a week with the dark earth of the valley, and this slightly high and muddy tonic invigorates the brown trout of the river.

I pluck a Spook from the felt page of a leather fly book — a fly which has probably not been used since the previous season, under the same circumstances. I slap the garish white pattern on the edges of the eddies, and the brown trout of 16 to 18 inches slash at the dart retrieve. The Spook catches 30 or 40 fish in an evening — rare abundance for so tough a stream; but it is the moment for the pattern.

Hook:	Mustad-Viking 9672; 4, 6, 8
Thread:	white 2/0 nylon
Tail:	matched slips of faint speckled white turkey wing quill
Butt:	medium red chenille
Body:	white wool
Ribbing:	3 or 4 turns of medium silver tinsel
Underwing:	sparse white calf tail fibers (length of the body and the tail)
Middlewing:	small bunch of mallard flank fibers
Overwing:	matched sections of speckled white

turkey feather (on each side
of the underwings)
Head: a thin rear band of natural grey deer
body hair (clipped to allow a flare of tips to
encircle the body). White deer
body hair spun to cover the remainder of
hook to the eye (clipped in a bullet shape).

Searcy's Muddler

This early Muddler variation is popular on coastal streams and desert lakes of Washington. It is listed in *Flies of the Pacific Northwest,* by Roy Patrick. A note in the book adds, "Seems we are getting into this type of head on fishing. As one customer said, 'Seems everyone is getting Muddler happy.' "

Hook:	Mustad-Viking 79580 (4X long); 2, 4, 6, 8, 10
Thread:	grey 2/0 nylon
Tail:	10 fibers of a pintail flank feather
Body:	dubbed muskrat fur
Ribbing:	oval gold tinsel
Underwing:	white calf tail hair and black skunk tail hair (mixed)
Overwing:	pintail flank fibers (on each side of the hair to the length of the body and the tail)
Head:	natural grey deer body hair (collar flair of tips)

(The clip-style of the head is not specified in *Flies of the Pacific Northwest,* but I prefer the pattern with a sparse shag cut, since I often dress the fly with a wrap of fine copper wire for weight.)

Gordon Dean — originated by Gordon Dean of New York City

The yellow version of the Muddler Minnow is an "exciter" pattern. It is a good fly for twitching through riffles of a rainbow stream.

Hook:	Mustad-Viking 9672; 8, 6, 10
Thread:	grey 2/0 nylon
Tail:	dyed yellow sections of white turkey quill
Body:	flat gold tinsel
Underwing:	sparse red calf tail hair and sparse yellow calf tail hair (mixed)
Overwing:	matched sections of dyed yellow turkey quill
Head:	natural grey deer body hair (clipped in a bullet taper)

Black Bear — tied by the Gapen Tackle Company

A natural sculpin is a creature of concealment, the color phase shading to match the predominant rocks of the river bed. In streams with pale bottoms, the fish bleaches to a tan-cream mottled hue (e.g., the South Fork of the Flathead). In rivers with dark bottoms, it splotches to an almost black speckle (e.g., the Firehole).

During rise-absent moments of a week on the Firehole, it was possible to pound the riffles productively with a minnow-type fly. Patterns were alternated — a Mickey Finn or a Dark Edson Tiger or a regular Muddler Minnow — but usually a No. 12 or No. 10 Black Bear nabbed rainbows and browns in consistent fashion.

I threaded among geiser potholes of hot water above the Iron Bridge, the angling almost too easy; and I strolled the shoreline at evening to pop the fast stretches of the river with a sparse Black Bear. The small bucktail tabbed bouncing trout of 14 to 17 inches every few casts on an across stream retrieve.

When I changed to a garish Purple Marabou Muddler, trout on the prowl, for some reason, even struck at the odd pattern. Fish leaped into the air for a clearer picture of the apparition or nipped repeatedly on a retrieve at the trailing wing of the fly, but not once did a trout hook up on the Marabou.

Typically, with underwater flies there are different patterns that provoke strikes. Often two greatly varying types of bucktail or streamer attract hits, but one of the patterns records a significant advantage in hooking trout — although not always so extreme as the Black Bear/Purple Marabou incidents.

The Black Bear is an alternate to a Muddler Minnow. In waters where the darker variation is a slightly better match for natural feed, the pattern is often slightly more effective for selective trout. The fish attack with a convinced intent — short striking often resulting from a slight discrepancy with the native minnow.

Hook:	Mustad-Viking 9672; 8, 10, 12
Thread:	grey 2/0 nylon
Tail:	black hair fibers (sparse)
Body:	flat gold tinsel
Underwing:	black hair fibers (sparse)
Overwing:	matched slips of black crow quill
Head:	natural grey deer body hair (trimmed shaggy)

Cock-Eyed Muddler

This less buoyant version of the Muddler type combines the swim action of the deer hair collar and the attraction of the jungle cock eye. With its absorbent chenille head, the pattern sinks easily to a 2 to 3-foot depth. Even without extra weighting on the shank, the fly works at the level of holding fish.

Ted Barbieri of Connecticut sent the pattern with the note, "This fly is excellent on Cape Cod for rainbows and sea-run browns. The results are fine in all sizes down to No. 12. It is also effective on Atlantic salmon when it is tied on the regular up-eye hook."

Hook:	Mustad-Viking 79580 (4X long);
	6, 8, 10, 12
Thread:	yellow 2/0 nylon
Tail:	matched slips of brown mottled turkey
Body:	flat gold tinsel
Undersing:	grey squirrel tail fibers
Overwing:	imitation jungle cock eye feathers
Collar:	spun deer hair (tips left in the flare
	backwards — stubs trimmed to the shank)
Head:	yellow chenille (wound in a tapered front
	in place of the clipped hair head)

SCULPIN IMITATIONS

Each spring, reservoir lakes in the mountains fill with snow melt run-off — the splash of excess water over the tops of the hydroelectric dams pushes a wash of immature spring-spawn fish tumbling to the spill basin. With precise timing for a specific river, the angler encounters an accessible bonanza of trout on the prowl.

Frank Johnson traveled to the Tongue River of eastern Montana to hit the stream at a prime moment. On a river little-known for trout, he caught in a single hour browns of 7 and 11 pounds with the Bullhead pattern. Frank noted on trips each spring to this river, "A man may not catch many fish, maybe two or three a day, but I've never seen a trout of less than four pounds from the gorge below the dam" — indeed, a worthy proposition for a gamble.

Streamside Bullhead — originated by Frank Johnson and Rich Anderson of Streamside Anglers

This fly serves as a realistic imitation of the *Cottus* sculpin, with a solid reputation as a "big trout" special. It is an alternate for the fly fisherman who wants to catch a trophy fish without resorting to live bait. Cast in a manner similar to a bait fisherman's sculpin drift, the fly is angled up and across to tumble downstream with a minimum of line pull.

Hook:	Mustad-Viking 79580 (4X long); 2, 4, 6, 8
Thread:	brown 2/0 nylon
Body:	dark tan wool (thick)
Ribbing:	oval gold tinsel
Overwing:	furnace rooster hackle (1 feather — flat over the back)
Head:	2 color banded — light brown at rear half; dark brown at forward half (bushy color — clipped in a flattened shape)

(The pattern is tied in a slightly slimmer line of shape than other sculpin imitations.)

Troth Bullhead

This fly was featured in the May, 1969 issue of the United Fly Tyers' Roundtable magazine.

233

> *Hook:* Mustad 36890 (turned-up looped oval eye
> — an Atlantic salmon hook);
> 3/0, 2/0, 1/0, 1
> *Thread:* black nylon, size D
> *Thread:* black nylon, size D
> *Tail:* skunk tail hair (mostly cream)
> *Body:* cream angora yarn (full)
> *Back:* black ostrich herl (tied in at the shoulder
> and at the bend of the hook)
> *Collar:* natural dear body hair (left mostly
> on the top and at the sides)
> *Head:* natural deer body hair — the top
> blackened with a felt-tip pen compressed
> and trimmed to a flat sculpin shape)

The disjointed swim of the Troth Bullhead copies the helpless drift of a sculpin. As it responds to the tumble of the current, the fly darts and dips into holding spots. A jumbo-size version of this pattern will milk the potential of swift water habitat.

Al Troth explained the technique of fishing the pattern, "You know where I use the Bullhead? I drift it in the runs maybe a few feet in depth. I put a split-shot on the leader near the eye, and I bounce it down the riffle. On a stream like the Madison, where the whole river is a shallow run, the fly hits those hidden pockets."

Flathead Sculpin — originated by George F. Grant (recipient of
the Buz Buszek award as outstanding flytier of
1973, presented by the Federation of Fly Fishermen)

This pattern, sent by George Grant, represented a bit of perfection. There was no intention of letting a mere fish mangle the Sculpin, the fly preserved in my personal collection. I fashioned copies of the original and retrieved these replicas in a tub of water to insure the same enticing undulation of swim achieved by the flattened body construction of the sample.

234

At a weight of nearly 14½ grains, the Flathead Sculpin is a superb deep-running sculpin imitation. The fly neither floats due to excessive deer hair nor wallows due to a non-planing head shape. It is a special pattern for use with a variety of sinking lines to probe bottom areas of large rivers.

Hook:	Mustad-Limerick 9575 (4X long); 2, 4
Thread:	yellow Nymo "A"
Tail:	fibers of a grey-green pheasant rump feather
Brass Pins:	¾ inch pleating pins (fastened at the sides of the hook shank)
Inner Core of Body:	yellow wool
Outer Body:	nylon-coated wire trolling line (.018)
Back Feather:	mottled green-tan-black pheasant body hackle (cemented flat on the back of the body)
Pectoral Fins:	mottled green-tan-black pheasant body hackle (curving outwards at the side of the body)
Head:	natural deer body hair — darkened on top with a felt-tip marker (trimmed in a V-shape)

Spuddler — originated by Red Monical and Don Williams; featured in Dan Bailey's mail-order catalog (which attains the status of a fly fishing reference volume)

In reminiscence, it is too tempting to make the fooling of trout an assured feat — in memory, it is too easy to gloss over the frustration of a dejected fisherman at a loss for another tactic. There are those days when an angler is helpless before the vagaries of fish (or as Graydon Fenn aptly warned prior to a day of scant fortune on the Beaverhead River, "Don't let anyone forget how to be humble with these trout!")

At the moment when hope has frittered away and final casts are mechanical exercises of futility, the Spuddler is unsnagged from the felt leaf of the fly book. The spool on the reel is changed to a sink-tip line. The leader is shortened to 6 feet, and the weighted pattern is soaked in the mouth.

The Spuddler as a mid-depth fly is the last-chance hope on a blank day. Under these tough conditions, it does not always catch trout. Often enough it does, however, when it is plied in the smaller sizes as a sculpin tid-bit at the resting spots of trout rather than at their feeding spots.

Hook:	Mustad-Viking 9672 (3X long); 8, 10, 12
Thread:	brown 2/0 nylon
Tail:	brown calf tail fibers
Body:	cream angora yarn
Underwing:	brown calf tail fibers (sparse)
Overwing:	4 grizzly hackle feathers dyed brown
Gills:	red wool (wrapped over the wing tie-off)
Carapice Hair:	red squirrel tail hair (spread in a cape over the top of the body)
Head:	brown antelope (slipped in a V-shape with a flat trim on the bottom)

Whitlock Sculpin — originated by Dave Whitlock;
    featured in the July 1968 issue of *Field & Stream* in the
    article "Match-the-Minnow Streamer Fly Series"

This pattern is an extremely realistic interpretation of the bulky shape of the sculpin. A problem with all Bullhead simulations is created by the large dense-spun head of deer hair. The buoyancy of its hollow fibers counteracts even the sink-power of liberal lead wrapping, but a simple trick is applicable to all sub-surface spun-hair patterns.

On a frustrating day on the Madison River, a client cast a Whitlock Sculpin. "Great," he hollered, "a fly that weighs a pound and floats a Hi-d sinking line."

The situation sparked the idea — increased lead weight was only a clumsy solution — of soaking a Sculpin pattern in a jar of water before a day of fishing. The hollow hair absorbed water, allowing the fly effective bottom presentation immediately. It water-logged quicker in the jar than during moments of fishing, since there was no air-drying in the pre-soak.

Hook:	Mustad-Viking 9672 (3X long); 2, 4, 6
Thread:	cream Nymo (body) — white A nylon
Body:	buff fox underfur (dubbed in a taper thickening towards the head)
Ribbing:	medium oval gold tinsel
Underwing:	red fox squirrel tail fibers and variegated Cree neck hackle fibers (small bunch)
Overwing:	three well-banded fan-like feathers from a hen pheasant; one tied flat over the underwing — others flared to each side to simulate large pectoral fins (red wool wrapped over the bulky tie-down area of thread)
Head:	deer hair dyed several shades of brown — spun in small bunches of varying color to achieve a banded effect (hair trimmed in a flattened bulk to represent the large head of the sculpin — rear band of hair tips formed as a collar hackle)

(The hook is weighted with wraps of .020 guage lead wire over the rear ⅔ of the shank.)

237

The Hair Sucker — An Imitative Pattern

The ubiquitous sucker is a common forage fish co-existing with trout in nearly all flows. The young brood of running-water species hide in the rock crevices of riffles, providing a weak-swimming prey often rooted from their sanctuaries; in late June, at the tail end of high water in the West, it is common to discover specimens in stomach samples from large trout.

There exist many attempted imitations of the common sucker. Usually bucktail flies are patterned along its color scheme; no doubt at moments these representations catch trout. It is suspected that these general patterns are not the ultimate simulation of a sucker, but rather are effective randomly because of the allure of the bucktail.

A young sucker moves with a swim-action like the sculpin's drift. The fish darts with a spurt of initial panic, but it possesses poor capacity for sustained mobility. The sucker wobbles feebly in the force of current, seeking only to gain the bottom calm. Concealment is its means of protection; escape is not a manner of survival.

Only the bulk of hair at the head of a fly simulates the feeble action of a sucker. A representative pattern combines the spun-hair head with a sparse silhouette of feathers placed horizontally on top of the hook. When it is wet, the fly is slimmer than the Muddler Minnow, tapering off from the shoulders to the smaller tail of an immature sucker.

> *Hook:* Mustad 36890 (turned-up looped eye —
> an Atlantic Salmon hook); size is matched
> to the young of the year brood
>
> *Thread:* grey 2/0 nylon
>
> *Tail:* 6 to 8 fibers of a pheasant tail feather
> (short length)

       Body: eggshell white yarn
   Ribbing: oval gold tinsel
Underwing: 2 dark olive hen feathers; tied flat on top
           of the shank to extend beyond the bend of hook
  Topwing: tip-feather of bronze dun marabou; tied on
           the edge — a short quill extending
           half-way down the shank —
             (The quills of both these wings
             are lashed to the shank with
             the gold tinsel — spiked
             Matuka fashion)
      Head: rear band — spun deer hair dyed a dark
           blood-red; a thin collar directly at the
           tie-off of the wing to spread a
           short wrap of fibers back around the
           body (clip the spun-stubs right
           down to the base)
           natural grey deer — body hair dyed a bronze dun —
           clipped shaggy on sides and on top, but trimmed
           flat on the bottom (spun sparse with a flare
           of tips extending beyond the flare of red tips —
           the different colors in combination form
           a prismatic imitation —
             (The pattern is weighted with lead
             strips lashed to the sides of
             the hook shank)

The Hair Sucker was tested by a network of angling cronies. Their suggestions were incorporated to produce the workable imitation, the effective molding only achieved by thinning bits of material until the finished fly was a slimmer variation of the Muddler Minnow — a result especially valuable for No. 14 to No. 8 hook sizes. The major angling in Montana consisted of flogging the Missouri River below Hauser Dam. Bill Seeples and I averaged a few trout over 4 pounds each evening. By word of mouth, the reputation of the fly spread to the regulars of the riverwhen we

239

answered the questions of curious anglers.

Russel Juel set up his fly tying equipment to supply the demand for the pattern. For a boom business in the evenings, he kept the finished flies soaking in a glass to water-log the deer hair. He dispensed them "ready-to-use" to anglers, selling over 170 samples of the fly within 7 days.

POSTSCRIPT

In a study of state streams, the Montana Fish & Game Department disclosed that, of 160 miles of channel studied, 24 miles of stream bed and 44 miles of stream bank had been man-altered.

The study further revealed, during electro-shock testing of the Ruby River fish populations, that bank alterations had caused a 61% reduction in trout population and that channel straightening had resulted in an 80% reduction.

A section of the East Gallatin River was used in the study to illustrate the amount of change in a particular stream bed:

    1937 — 6.12 miles
    1954 — 4.30 miles
    1964 — 3.65 miles

These figures represent, over 27 years, a 40% diminishing of length and a 68% increase in slope.

These facts chronicle a horror story of state environmental irresponsibility. The once fabled Montana trout streams are not only deteriorating — they are disappearing.

To help prevent further stream destruction, please support environmental action.

Gary LaFontaine
Deer Lodge, Montana
December 1976

241

Bibliography

The titles of many angling books are mentioned in the text and in the footnotes; not only do these references serve as endorsement of the books' contents, but the titles, listed below, offer the reader a valuable general fly fishing bibliography.

Bates, Joseph D., *Streamer Fly Tying and Fishing;* The Stackpole Company; 1966.

Bergman, Ray, *Trout;* Alfred A. Knopf; 3rd edition 1975.

Brooks, Charles, *The Trout and the Stream;* Crown Publishers; 1974.

Caucci, Al and Nastasi, Bob, *Hatches;* Comparahatch Publishing; 1974.

Hewitt, Edward Ringling, *A Trout and Salmon Fisherman for 75 Years;* Van Cortlandt Press; 2nd edition 1972.

Jennings, Preston, *A Book of Trout Flies;* Crown Publishers; 2nd edition 1970.

LaBranche, George, *The Dry Fly and Fast Water;* Van Cortlandt Press; 2nd edition 1972.

Leonard, J. Edson, *Flies;* A. S. Barnes and Company, Inc; 1950.

Marinaro, Vincent C., *Modern Dry Fly Code;* Crown Publishers; 2nd edition 1970.

Schwiebert, Ernest, *Nymphs;* Winchester Press; 1973.

Swisher, Doug and Richards, Carl, *Selective Trout;* Crown Publishers; 1971.